GEOLOGIC TRIPS

San Francisco
and the Bay Area

Ted Konigsmark

1998

GeoPress

Gualala California

Geologic Trips
San Francisco and the Bay Area

© 1998 by Ted Konigsmark

Unless indicated otherwise, all photographs and illustrations in this book are by the author. The cover photograph is the Golden Gate Bridge from East Fort Baker.

Use caution and common sense while on the geologic trips. Drive, park and hike safely. Do not go along the seashore when conditions are potentially dangerous, and do not go anywhere that you feel may be unsafe. On inland trails, try to avoid the ubiquitous poison oak. Changes by man or nature can occur along any of the roads, hiking trails, and especially along the shoreline. The information contained in this book is correct to the best of the author's knowledge at the date of publication. The author and publisher assume no liability for accidents, injury, or any losses by individuals or groups using this publication.

Library of Congress Catalog Card Number: 97-94461

ISBN 0-9661316-4-9

GeoPress
P.O. Box 964
Gualala, CA 95445

PREFACE

Although I am a native Californian and received much of my geologic training in California, I spent most of my geologic career elsewhere, mainly involved with oil exploration research and in oil exploration in South America and Southeast Asia. After retiring a few years ago, I returned with my wife to live in California. Upon my return, I found that the rocks in California had not changed while I was gone, but that the geologic understanding of the rocks had changed dramatically. Rocks that had once been complex and mysterious could now be explained in relatively simple terms, thanks to the many new concepts that had grown out of the theory of plate tectonics during the last thirty years.

Upon returning to California, I also found that many of my nongeologist neighbors had a keen interest in learning about the rocks that make up the sea cliffs and hillsides of the coastal area where we live. In response to this interest, I recently published a small book, *Geologic Trips, Sea Ranch*, about the geology of this area. Since the book was well received, it seemed to me that there might be interest for a similar book that would explain the geology of the San Francisco area. San Francisco has classic exposures of some unusual rocks called the *Franciscan* that were formed during a collision of continents from 65 to 175 million years ago. No other major city in the world has a greater variety of unusual and rare rocks that are easily accessible for observation. San Francisco is also a good laboratory from which to examine the nearby San Andreas and Hayward faults, which have left their indelible imprint on the city in many ways.

Many geologists have contributed to our understanding of the geology of the Coast Ranges, the San Andreas fault, the Franciscan rocks, and to the geology of the San Francisco area. I have drawn freely on their work in preparing this book. Without their work this book would not have been possible. For brevity and simplicity, I have not referenced these sources in the text, but a number of excellent publications are listed in the section on Further Reading. These references are highly recommended for anyone who wants more detail on the geology of the San Francisco area and the Coast Ranges.

CONTENTS

Part II. The Geologic Trips (cont.)

The hills of downtown San Francisco are framed by the Golden Gate Bridge in this view from the Marin Headlands.

A GEOLOGIC VIEW
OF SAN FRANCISCO

For a spectacular view of San Francisco, go to Battery 129 in the Marin Headlands west of the Golden Gate Bridge. To the west is the open Pacific. To the south is the San Francisco Peninsula, with steep sea cliffs from Cliff House through Lands End to Fort Point at the south end of the Golden Gate Bridge. Beyond the Golden Gate Bridge you can see the many hills of downtown San Francisco dotted with buildings and houses. San Francisco Bay broadens out to the east of the Golden Gate, holding Alcatraz Island and Angel Island in its outstretched hand. To the southeast, the Bay Bridge steps across San Francisco Bay to Oakland, and the Berkeley Hills and Oakland Hills lie in the background. Beneath you are the majestic cliffs and small bays that are characteristic of the Marin Headlands, with assorted red, green, and yellow rocks.

This landscape didn't just happen. It's the product of geological processes that have been going on for nearly two hundred million years. The land is made up of a number of different types of rocks, and these rocks have been shaped by earth movements and erosional processes to form the landscape that you now see. During the geologic trips in and around San Francisco, you will discover why these rocks now form the hills, bays, islands, and peninsulas of the Bay Area.

The rocks that underlie San Francisco are referred to by geologists as the *Franciscan* rocks. Like the residents of San Francisco, some of the Franciscan rocks have traveled thousands of miles across the Pacific, whereas others are homegrown. Some are common rocks, and others are very unusual or have undergone such drastic changes that their original character is unknown.

Although the Franciscan rocks are varied, they do have one thing in common. They all met and were squeezed together in the Franciscan subduction zone. This subduction zone resulted from a long, slow, grinding collision between two giant plates that once covered a major part of the earth's surface. The Coast Ranges of California are formed from the wreckage of this collision. San Francisco lies in the middle of this wreckage and is an excellent place to poke around and do a postmortem on the collision.

HOW TO USE THIS BOOK

This book is written for the nongeologist and describes seven geologic trips that will give the reader an understanding of the rocks, faults, earthquakes, and landforms of San Francisco and the Bay Area. The book is divided into two parts. Part I provides some geologic background material useful to the nongeologist. The nongeologist should look over this material before going on the geologic trips in order to make the trips more meaningful and enjoyable — especially the sections on Geologic Thinking, Plate Tectonics, and California Faults and Earthquakes.

Part II gives a detailed description of the geologic trips. During each of the trips, you will visit specific geologic sites where the local geology will be discussed and illustrated with maps and/or photographs. Each trip is planned to emphasize a different aspect of the geology of the San Francisco area. All of the geologic sites that you will visit are on land that is open to the public. Most of the sites involve short, easy walks, but nothing really strenuous. Most of the geologic sites are also in scenic areas and have other attractions as well as the rocks. Allow time to enjoy the scenery, visit these other attractions, and perhaps have a picnic.

Most of the geologic trips can be made from San Francisco by car and will take half a day to a day. However, two days should be allowed for the trip to the Point Reyes Peninsula. Ferries are used on the trips to Alcatraz and Angel Islands. The ferry to Alcatraz leaves from Fisherman's Wharf, and this trip can easily be done in two or three hours. The ferry to Angel Island leaves from Tiburon. A full day should be allowed for this trip, since the trip involves a delightful hike around the circumference of the island.

I have tried to minimize the use of the more technical geologic terms in this book. Nonetheless, many of these terms are required to communicate the geologic story in a reasonably efficient manner. The Glossary at the end of the book will help you sort out and understand these terms.

PART I

GEOLOGIC BACKGROUND

GEOLOGIC THINKING

To better understand the rocks and the geologic processes that you will be seeing on the geologic trips, you need to pause and learn a new way of thinking. You need to think like a geologist. This thinking process is not necessarily difficult — just different. Here are some guidelines:

<u>Listen to the Rocks:</u> When looking at the rocks exposed in a roadcut, on a mountainside, or along the shoreline, try to erase, in your mind, the present landscape. When the rocks were formed, the landscape was completely different. Look at the rocks and let them tell you what the landscape was like when the rocks were formed. If the rocks were formed at the bottom of a large ocean, imagine yourself standing on the bottom of that ocean, far from any land. If there are several different types of rocks in the outcrop, each type may tell a different story. The rocks changed as the landscape changed. To understand the geologic history of the area, the geologist must piece these stories together, like reading an old tattered book with many missing pages.

<u>Geologic Time:</u> Most people think in terms of years and decades and consider that a century is a long time. Geologists think in terms of millions and hundreds of millions of years. When you think in millions of years, enormous changes can be made in the landscape even with very slow geologic processes. If you compared the 4.6-billion-year age of the earth to the age of a 100-year-old man, you would find that northern California did not exist until the man was 95 years old. The Coast Ranges began to form when he was 99 years old, and the Pleistocene Ice Ages took place two weeks before his 100th birthday. The 2-million-year period of the Ice Ages — during which time the Sierras were uplifted several thousands of feet and humans evolved — is only an eye-flick in geologic time.

<u>Uplift and Subsidence:</u> The surface of the earth is in constant movement. Some areas are moving up, some are subsiding, and some are moving laterally. These movements may be from a few feet to several thousand feet in a million years. Over time, these movements can uplift rocks that

were once buried at depths of more than 30 miles and expose the rocks at the surface of the earth. The movements can also cause subsidence of rocks that were formed at the earth's surface to depths of more than 30 miles as younger and younger rocks are piled on top of older rocks.

Scale: Although upward and downward movements of the earth's surface of 30 or more miles may seem large, these movements are not large when compared to the size of the earth. If the earth were the size of a basketball, an uplift of 30,000 feet on the earth's surface would be equivalent to the thickness of a sheet of paper on the surface of the basketball, a slight imperfection on the basketball.

To most people, a mountain range such as the Rocky Mountains seems very large, and the rocks that make up the mountain range appear very hard and brittle. Indeed, many of these rocks are used as building stones. However, compared to the size of the earth, these seemingly strong and brittle rocks can easily bend over distances of tens or hundreds of miles and form giant folds like a rumpled table cloth. One must think big, and recognize that the rocks that make up the earth behave in a different manner when viewed on a large scale.

Erosion and Deposition: When rocks are uplifted above sea level, they are attacked by many different types of weathering and erosional processes. These processes include rivers, landslides, wind, glaciers, waves, bulldozers, plants, animals, bacteria, and humans. These weathering and erosional processes break down the hard rocks of the mountains into sediments — boulders, pebbles, sand, silt, and clay. Rivers then carry these sediments to the oceans. Over millions of years of time, entire mountain ranges can be worn down to sea level by these weathering and erosional processes.

The sediments carried by the rivers to the oceans are deposited in sedimentary basins. Sedimentary basins are low spots on the ocean floor that occur where the surface of the earth is subsiding. This process of uplift and erosion of mountains, and subsidence and filling of sedimentary basins, has been going on for hundreds of millions of years and continues today. The locations of these uplifts and subsidences change with time. Sedimentary basins can be uplifted to form mountain ranges, and mountain ranges can be worn down to become the floor of sedimentary basins.

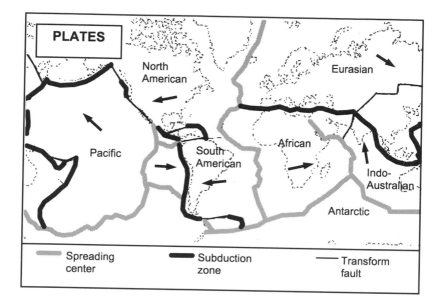

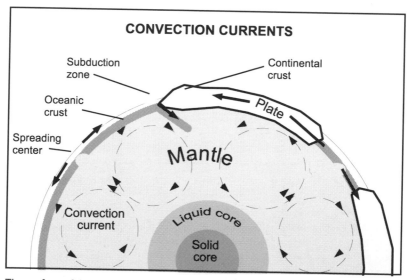

The surface of the earth is covered by a dozen or so large rigid plates. These plates are carried in different directions by convection currents within the earth's mantle. The movement of the plates and the deformation of the rocks along the plate boundaries are referred to as plate tectonics.

PLATE TECTONICS

For decades, geologists had struggled with attempts to explain the unusual and diverse rocks that make up the Franciscan. It was not until the theory of plate tectonics evolved about thirty years ago that real progress was made in understanding the Franciscan. According to the theory of plate tectonics the surface of the earth is made up of a number of large plates that are slowly moving in different directions, propelled by convection currents deep within the earth. In some places, the plates are torn apart by the convection currents. In other places, the plates collide or scrape by one another with glancing blows. The rocks in the contact zones between the plates are deformed in different ways depending on whether the plates are being pulled apart, are colliding, or slipping by one another.

The mechanics of plate tectonics are relatively simple. The plates are about 60 miles thick and consist of rocks that are cool, light weight, and brittle. These rocks tend to break rather than bend when subjected to large stress. In contrast, the rocks below the plates are very hot, very heavy, and dark. These rocks, called the *mantle*, extend to the core of the earth and are at such high temperatures and pressures that they do not break, but flow when subjected to large stress. This ability to flow enables the rocks in the mantle to form large *convection cells* in which the hot parts of the mantle rise and the cool parts descend. When a convection cell comes into contact with an overlying plate, it pulls the plate in the direction that the current is moving. Rising convection currents diverge and pull the overlying plates apart. Descending currents converge and cause the overlying plates to collide. Convection currents may also move past one another horizontally and drag adjacent plates in opposite directions.

Spreading centers form where plates pull apart, *subduction zones* form where plates collide, and *transform faults* form where plates slip by one another horizontally. We see evidences of all three of these types of plate contacts in the Franciscan rocks. Let's now take a closer look at what happens along these spreading centers, subduction zones and transform faults.

Spreading Centers

Spreading centers form where rising convection cells spread out horizontally and pull the overlying plates in opposite directions. The hot rocks in the earth's mantle move upward into the area between the spreading plates and the rocks melt due to the lower pressure near the surface. The molten rock forms a magma chamber along the spreading center a mile or so below the earth's surface. From time to time the magma flows out from the magma chamber onto the sea floor and solidifies as basalt. As the plates continue to move apart, new basalt is manufactured at the spreading center and the older basalt moves away from the spreading center in opposite directions, as if on diverging conveyer belts. The ocean floor thus becomes larger and larger as spreading continues.

This process of manufacturing ocean floor from spreading centers has been going on for hundreds of millions of years and is still in progress. The rift valleys of Africa, which include Lake Malawi, Lake Tanganyika and Lake Albert, represent the early phase of a spreading center. The African continent is being torn apart along these rift valleys. If this spreading continues, the African rift valleys will be become a small ocean basin similar to the Red Sea. With further spreading, this small ocean basin would become larger, like the Atlantic Ocean, and perhaps eventually as large as the Pacific. All of the world's major ocean basins have been formed by sea floor spreading in this manner and are underlain by basaltic rocks that were formed at spreading centers.

New ocean floor is typically formed along the spreading centers at rates of from one to five inches per year. If you translate these spreading rates into geologic time, it is obvious that enormous areas of sea floor have been manufactured in relatively short periods of time. At an average spreading rate of two inches per year, a spreading center would manufacture 32 miles of ocean floor in one million years, or 3200 miles of ocean floor in 100 million years. An entire ocean basin as large as the Pacific could easily be formed within 200 million years. Indeed, the oldest oceanic floor anywhere in the world is in the western Pacific and is less than 200 million years old. At these rates, oceanic floor would rapidly cover the entire surface of the globe. However, this does not happen because oceanic rocks are being consumed in subduction zones at about the same rate that they are being manufactured in spreading centers.

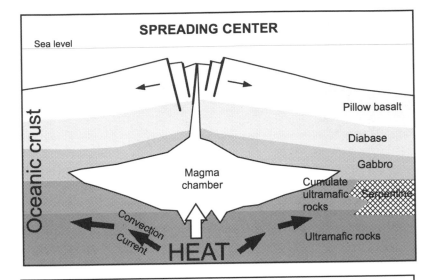

Oceanic Crust

Oceanic crust is typically about five miles thick and is made up of several distinct rock units: 1) U*ltramafic rocks* in the lower part of the lithosphere are melted by hot rising convection currents and form a magma chamber at the spreading center. 2) Pyroxene and olivine crystals form in the magma chamber as the magma is cooled by the adjacent rocks. The pyroxene and olivine crystals then fall through the magma like snowflakes and accumulate on the floor of the magma chamber as the *cumulate ultramafic.* 3) As iron and magnesium are removed from the magma by crystallization of the pyroxene and olivine, the composition of the remaining magma changes, and the magma becomes richer in calcium, sodium, potassium, aluminum, and silica. From time to time this lighter magma flows out onto the sea floor and forms *pillow basalt.* 4) As the plates move away from the spreading center, the magma that remained in the magma chamber becomes cooler and crystallizes into *gabbro.* 5) D*iabase* forms from magma that cooled and solidified in feeder cracks before it flowed out onto the sea floor as pillow basalt. 6) S*erpentine* forms when sea water enters fractures that are formed at the spreading center and reacts with the ultramafic and cumulate ultramafic rocks to form complex hydrated iron-magnesium silicates.

Subduction Zones

Subduction zones occur where descending convection currents in the mantle cause the overlying plates to collide and one plate is carried beneath the other plate. Many of the major geographic features of the earth's surface have been formed along subduction zones, including mountain ranges, island arcs, volcanos, and deep oceanic trenches. To understand what happens when plates collide, let's look at the composition of the plates in more detail.

The huge plates that cover the surface of the earth consist mainly of two different types of rocks, *oceanic* and *continental*. Some plates are mainly oceanic rocks, some mainly continental rocks, and some plates have rocks of both types. The oceanic rocks are formed at spreading centers and represent the cold, hardened skin of the earth's mantle, with some minor chemical changes. In contrast, the continental rocks consist mainly of lighter-colored, lighter-weight *granitic* rocks that are rich in the light elements. Continental rocks are made in subduction zones, as will be described shortly. Since the continental rocks are relatively light, they float on the heavy fluid-like rocks of the earth's mantle like marshmallows on cocoa. The oceanic rocks also float on the mantle, but lower, like the skim of the cocoa.

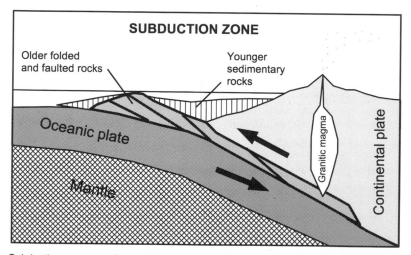

Subduction zones are formed along the collision zones between plates. In this subduction zone an oceanic plate is being subducted below a continental plate. Granitic magma is being formed by melting of the rocks in the subduction zone. Some of the granitic magma is making its way to the surface to form a volcano, and some will cool more slowly below the surface to become granite.

There are three types of plate collisions, and each type has different consequences on the rocks that form in the related subduction zone. A continental plate may collide with an oceanic plate, two oceanic plates may collide, or two continental plates may collide. This is what happens during these collisions:

1. Where an oceanic plate collides with a continental plate, the heavier oceanic plate is *subducted* under the lighter continental plate. This subduction process thickens the lithosphere in the subduction zone. The thickened lithosphere rises isostatically and forms a chain of mountains. Most of the world's major mountain ranges, such as the Alps, Andes and the Cascades, have been formed in this manner. Earthquakes also occur along the subduction zones, caused by the rubbing of the plates as one plate is carried beneath the other. As the rocks in the subducted oceanic plate sink deeper into the earth's interior, some of the rocks become hot and melt to form magma. This magma is rich in light elements obtained from the melting of the wet sediments on the seafloor that were carried into the subduction zone. The magma is lighter than the surrounding rocks and therefore rises as a bulbous mass into the upper plate. If the magma reaches the surface it erupts as a volcano, like Mt. Rainier and Lassen Peak. The magma that doesn't reach the surface forms large magma chambers in the continental plate several miles below the surface. This magma cools slowly, and crystallizes into granite, like the granite in the Sierras. Over time, this process has manufactured the light granitic rocks that make up the continents that we live on.

2. Where two oceanic plates collide, one plate is subducted below the other, the lithosphere is thickened, and an island arc is formed. Most of the rocks in the oceanic plates are relatively dense, so that the mountains formed along the island arcs are not very high. The earthquakes are of moderate size, and the igneous rocks that are formed are intermediate in composition between granite and gabbro. The Caribbean Islands and Aleutian Islands are examples of island arcs formed along collision zones between oceanic plates.

3. Where two continental plates collide, one continental plate is forced below the other. Since both plates consist of thick and light rocks, the crust is abnormally thick along the subduction zone and very high mountains are formed. The Himalayan Mountain range was formed in this manner along the collision zone between the continental rocks in the Indo-Australian plate and the continental rocks of the Eurasian plate.

Transform Faults

Where convection currents cause one plate to slip by another plate horizontally, the zone along which this movement takes place is called a transform fault. These faults transform plate movement from one spreading center to another. A spreading center such as the East Pacific Rise is not a single continuous break in the earth's surface, but instead, consists of a number of spreading segments connected by transform faults. Since each side of the transform fault is on a different plate, each side moves in an opposite direction. At an average rate of a couple of inches per year the total amount of lateral movement can be large, as much as 300 miles in 10 million years.

Most transform faults are on oceanic plates and therefore not easily seen because they are covered by oceans. However, in some places, transform faults cut across continents. The San Andreas fault is a large transform fault that cuts across south and central California. The San Andreas fault transforms spreading movement from the East Pacific Rise spreading center in the Gulf of California to the Juan de Fuca Ridge spreading center off the coast of Oregon.

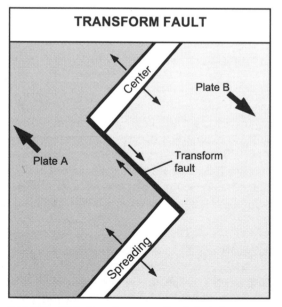

Transform faults form the connecting links between spreading centers and transform plate movement from one spreading center to another. Plates move past each other horizontally along transform faults.

Terranes

Continental plates are constantly being torn apart and moved by convection cells. Broken pieces of the plates may be carried hundreds or even thousands of miles. Eventually, these pieces are swept into a subduction zone somewhere and plastered onto a larger plate. These broken pieces of continents are called *terranes*. All of our continents are made up of numerous terranes that have been patched together like a crazy quilt. The continents are being recycled.

California is made up of a number of terranes that have been plastered along the western margin of North America over the last several hundred million years. Sonomia was added about 375 million years ago and Smartville about 225 million years ago. The Franciscan rocks, which began to be added to North America about 175 million years ago, consist of a number of smaller terranes. These terranes were carried northward and eastward to North America by plate movement and then left at the western doorstep of North America like a heap of discarded mice. Some terranes are separated by suture zones that consist of heavy, dark rocks called ophiolites. The ophiolites are remnants of the oceanic rocks that once separated the terranes.

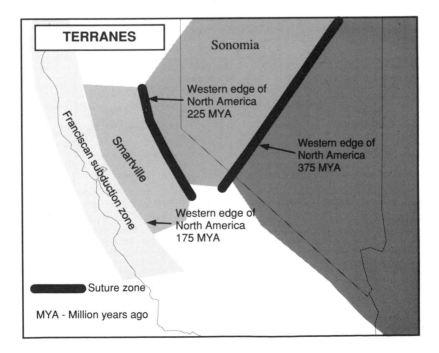

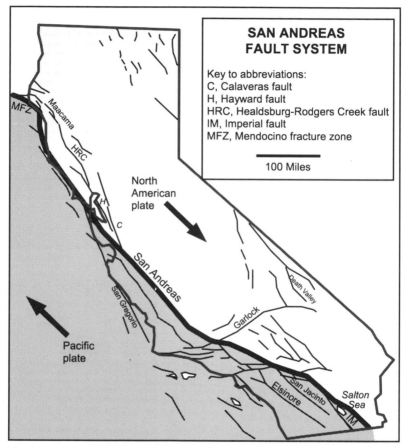

The San Andreas fault is a transform fault that forms part of the boundary between the North American plate and the Pacific plate. The fault extends from the Gulf of California northwest 750 miles to Cape Mendocino. Rocks on the west side of the fault have been carried north several hundred miles relative to rocks on the east side of the fault. The movement between the plates takes place along a number of faults in addition to the San Andreas, and these related faults are collectively referred to as the San Andreas fault system.

CALIFORNIA FAULTS AND EARTHQUAKES

San Andreas Fault System

Most earthquakes occur along the boundaries between the huge plates that cover the surface of the earth. As the plates move, they gouge, scrape, tear, buckle and fracture the brittle rocks along the edges of the plates. When the rocks break, shock waves travel through the rocks and cause earthquakes.

The San Andreas fault is a transform fault that forms the boundary between the Pacific plate, which is moving north, and the North American plate, which is moving west. California is slowly being torn apart along the San Andreas fault. The parts of California to the west of the fault, including San Diego, Los Angeles, Monterey, Santa Cruz and the Point Reyes Peninsula, are moving north at a rate of one to two inches per year relative to the remainder of California. California is, in fact, realizing its life-long dream of dividing into two separate parts, albeit not in the manner envisioned by most politicians.

Although most of the plate movement takes place along the San Andreas fault, some movement also occurs along a number of closely related faults that lie within 100 miles or so of the San Andreas fault. Most of these faults trend northwest, and in most the west side of the fault is moving north, just like the San Andreas. This group of faults is commonly referred to as the San Andreas fault system. The San Andreas fault system includes such local faults as the Hayward, Calaveras, Healdsburg-Rodgers Creek, Pilarcitos, and San Gregorio. Most all of the major earthquakes in California are caused by the San Andreas fault and nearby faults that are part of the San Andreas fault system.

The San Andreas fault formed about 25 million years ago when the East Pacific Rise spreading center reached the Franciscan subduction zone and began to be subducted under the North American plate. As the spreading center was subducted, the Farallon plate continued to be carried deep below the North American plate. However, the Pacific plate was moving in the opposite direction from the Farallon plate, and this caused problems in the subduction zone. Suddenly the rocks on the leading edge of the North American plate were no longer colliding with the Farallon plate, but instead were being pulled in the opposite direction by the Pacific plate. The portion of the North American plate that overlay the Pacific plate began to move northwest with the Pacific plate. The San Andreas fault formed to accommodate this movement.

There have been many attempts to determine the total amount of movement along the San Andreas fault. Ideally, to make this determination one would like to have a unique geologic feature displaced so that one part, like the head of a dinosaur, was on one side of the fault and the other part, the tail, was on the other side. By matching the head and tail it would be possible to document the exact amount of movement that had taken place. There have been several correlations of this type using similar rocks found on opposite sides of the fault, rather than pieces of a dinosaur. Most of these correlations suggest horizontal movement of at least 200 miles for the San Andreas fault in the San Francisco area. This would represent an average rate of movement of about one-half inch per year. It appears likely that significant additional movement took place along several of the other faults in the San Andreas fault system. The total movement between the plates is believed to be in the range of two inches per year. Indications are that there was even more movement on the San Andreas fault in southern California, perhaps 400 miles or more.

FAULT OFFSETS			
Movement	Millions of years		
(inches/yr.)	1	10	25
0.1	1.6 miles	16 miles	40 miles
0.5	8 miles	80 miles	200 miles
1.0	16 miles	160 miles	400 miles
2.0	32 miles	320 miles	800 miles

Small fault displacements over long periods of time can result in very large displacements.
Creep on the Hayward fault is about 0.2"/year.
Depending on location, the San Andreas fault is moving at about 0.5" to 2.0"/ year.

ORIGIN
San Andreas Fault

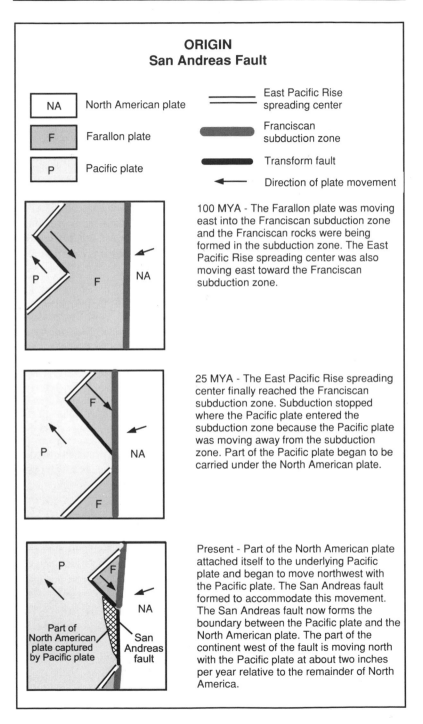

NA	North American plate
F	Farallon plate
P	Pacific plate

East Pacific Rise spreading center

Franciscan subduction zone

Transform fault

Direction of plate movement

100 MYA - The Farallon plate was moving east into the Franciscan subduction zone and the Franciscan rocks were being formed in the subduction zone. The East Pacific Rise spreading center was also moving east toward the Franciscan subduction zone.

25 MYA - The East Pacific Rise spreading center finally reached the Franciscan subduction zone. Subduction stopped where the Pacific plate entered the subduction zone because the Pacific plate was moving away from the subduction zone. Part of the Pacific plate began to be carried under the North American plate.

Present - Part of the North American plate attached itself to the underlying Pacific plate and began to move northwest with the Pacific plate. The San Andreas fault formed to accommodate this movement. The San Andreas fault now forms the boundary between the Pacific plate and the North American plate. The part of the continent west of the fault is moving north with the Pacific plate at about two inches per year relative to the remainder of North America.

Part of North American plate captured by Pacific plate

San Andreas fault

Earthquakes

Earthquakes occur when the rocks along a fault suddenly break and move. This sudden movement is transmitted through the earth as sharp vibrations that shake the rocks as they travel through the rocks. A small break will result in minor shaking and a large break will result in violent shaking. The amount of shaking is greatest near the break and rapidly decreases away from the break.

Two types of waves are formed when the rocks break — compressional waves and shear waves. The compressional waves, also known as primary or P waves, travel through the rocks like a sound wave through air, compressing the rocks ahead and stretching the rocks behind. They travel at a speed of 3.1 to 3.7 miles per second. The shear waves, also known as secondary or S waves, travel through the earth by moving the rocks laterally, like shaking a long rope. S waves travel at about 2.0 miles per second, so they reach an observer after the P waves.

When the P and S waves reach the surface of the earth, two new types of waves are formed, Raleigh waves and Love waves, and these waves travel along the earth's surface. The Raleigh waves travel like ripples on the surface of a pond, moving the surface of the earth up and down. The Love waves shake the ground laterally. It is these two sets of waves that cause most of the shaking and damage in an earthquake. Where rocks are solid and hard, the earthquake waves travel fast and shaking is minimized. In soft, unconsolidated rocks the waves travel slowly and the shaking is maximized, like shaking a bowl of Jell-O.

Most earthquake damage occurs in areas of soft, unconsolidated sediments. Three things can happen when earthquake waves reach these areas, and all are bad. First, the intensity of the shaking is magnified, perhaps by an order of magnitude or more. Secondly, the shaking settles the loose grains in the unconsolidated sediments, so that the surface of the ground can settle from several inches to over a foot, like cornflakes settling in a box. Lastly, where fine, unconsolidated sediments are saturated with water, some of the water is squeezed out from between the sand grains as the grains settle. This water rises to the top of the unconsolidated sediments and forms a lubrication layer that allows the overlying structures to settle or slip downslope, as if on a giant waterslide. This process is called liquefaction. During liquefaction water may flow up through cracks in pavement or asphalt and form small craters or volcanos. Major damage can be done far from an earthquake epicenter in areas susceptible to liquefaction.

The size of an earthquake is usually measured by the Richter scale (M) or the Modified Mercalli Intensity scale (MMI). The Richter scale measures the intensity of the earthquake based on seismograph records. The scale ranges from small magnitude M1.0 earthquakes, to "great" M8.0 earthquakes. The scale is logarithmic. For a one-unit increase in the scale there is a ten-fold increase in ground motion and a thirty-fold increase in energy released. An earthquake of M7.0 is ten times more violent than an earthquake of M6.0. This scale is used in many scientific studies of earthquakes.

RICHTER SCALE	
1	Not felt
2	May be felt
3	Slight damage
4	Moderate damage
5	Considerable damage
6	Severe damage
7	"Major", widespread damage
8	"Great", tremendous damage

The Modified Mercalli Intensity scale (MMI) measures the intensity of the earthquake based on damage to structures. This scale is used for detailed analysis of earthquake damage and also where good seismograph records are not available. The MMI scale uses Roman numerals I through XII and thus can be readily distinguished from the Richter scale.

MODIFIED MERCALLI INTENSITY SCALE	
I	Not generally felt
II	Suspended objects may swing
III	Hanging objects swing
IV	Dishes and doors disturbed
V	Very weak: small objects upset
VI	Weak: dishes broken
VII	Mild: strongly felt but little damage
VIII	Moderate: numerous chimneys fall
IX	Heavy: general panic, unreinforced masonry buildings collapse
X	Extreme: many frame structures destroyed
XI	Few masonry structures remain standing
XII	Damage nearly total

Major California Earthquakes

It takes a huge break, probably through the entire crust, to cause an earthquake of M8.0 or greater. A break of this magnitude would normally extend from tens to hundreds of miles along the fault, and the rocks along the fault would be offset tens of feet. Earthquakes of this size are very effective in releasing stress and it takes a long time for stress to build up again that would cause another M8.0 earthquake. Fortunately, these earthquakes are infrequent.

Earthquakes of M7.0 are typically accompanied by offsets of several feet over a distance of several tens of miles along the fault. These earthquakes can cause severe damage over wide areas. Earthquakes of M6.0 may or may not have breakage along the surface of the ground. However, if an earthquake of this size occurs in a metropolitan area, like the 1994 Northridge Earthquake (M6.7) in Los Angeles, it could still provide quite a jolt.

After a large earthquake there are normally a large number of aftershocks, smaller earthquakes in the vicinity of the original earthquake. The aftershocks are caused by adjustments of the rocks along the fault plane to the new stresses caused by the initial rupture. The largest aftershock is normally about one magnitude smaller than the main shock and the shocks become smaller and more numerous with time until they die out.

In California, there have been 66 earthquakes greater than M6.0 over the last 200 years. Of these, 47 were from M6.0 to M6.9; 16 were from M7.0 to M7.9; and three were greater than M8.0. The most recent earthquake in California greater than M8.0 was the Great San Francisco Earthquake of 1906 (M8.3). The other two "great" earthquakes were the Owens Valley Earthquake of 1872 (M8.3) and the 1857 Fort Tejon Earthquake (M8.3), over 100 years ago.

EARTHQUAKE SIZES	
Magnitude (Richter scale)	Average number of earthquakes worldwide per year
M 8.0	2
M 7.0	20
M 6.0	100
M 5.0	3,000
M 4.0	15,000

Small earthquakes are much more common than large earthquakes. Whereas there are many thousands of earthquakes worldwide each year that are smaller than M6.0, there are only 100 or so that are M6.0, about 20 that are M7.0, and about two that are M8.0 or larger.

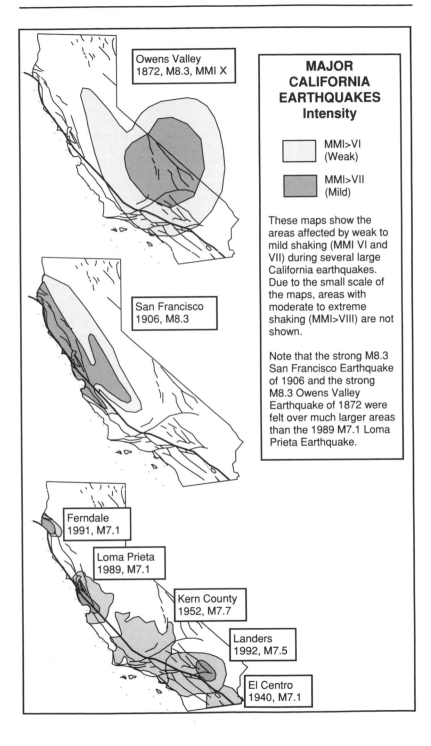

Owens Valley
1872, M8.3, MMI X

MAJOR CALIFORNIA EARTHQUAKES
Intensity

MMI>VI (Weak)

MMI>VII (Mild)

These maps show the areas affected by weak to mild shaking (MMI VI and VII) during several large California earthquakes. Due to the small scale of the maps, areas with moderate to extreme shaking (MMI>VIII) are not shown.

Note that the strong M8.3 San Francisco Earthquake of 1906 and the strong M8.3 Owens Valley Earthquake of 1872 were felt over much larger areas than the 1989 M7.1 Loma Prieta Earthquake.

San Francisco
1906, M8.3

Ferndale
1991, M7.1

Loma Prieta
1989, M7.1

Kern County
1952, M7.7

Landers
1992, M7.5

El Centro
1940, M7.1

Major Bay Area Earthquakes

The Bay Area is dissected by a number of major faults that are part of the San Andreas fault system. The most active of these faults are the San Andreas, Calaveras, and Hayward. San Francisco Bay lies in a depression formed between the Hayward and San Andreas faults.

Since the early 1800's, there have been eighteen earthquakes of M6.0 or greater in the Bay Area. These earthquakes are shown on the accompanying map. Four of these earthquakes were on the San Andreas fault, three on the Hayward fault, and two on the Calaveras fault. The other nine earthquakes were on smaller or previously unknown faults.

We'll look at two of these earthquakes in more detail as an indication of what might happen during a large Bay Area earthquake. The 1906 San Francisco Earthquake provides an example of the largest earthquake that would be expected. An earthquake of this size might occur once every 100 to 200 years or so. The Loma Prieta Earthquake of 1989 provides an example of a somewhat smaller earthquake. Earthquakes of this size might be expected once every few decades.

The Great San Francisco Earthquake of 1906: The Great San Francisco Earthquake struck San Francisco at 5:12 AM on April 18, 1906. The epicenter of the earthquake was a few miles west of San Francisco on the section of the San Andreas fault between Mussel Rock and the Point Reyes Peninsula. During the earthquake, the rocks along the San Andreas fault were broken for a distance of 280 miles from San Juan Bautista to Cape Mendocino. Rocks were offset as much as 21 feet along the fracture. Intense shaking lasted for 40 to 60 seconds. The estimated Richter magnitude was M8.3.

In San Francisco, many buildings collapsed or were heavily damaged by the quake. Most of this damage was in the area south of Market Street and in the Mission District, Financial District, and North Beach. The new City Hall collapsed. Streets buckled, cable car lines were bent, chimneys and exterior walls fell, and many windows in the city were shattered. Gas pipelines and water mains were also broken. Although many residents were thrown from their beds, this initial quake damage was relatively minor. The greatest damage was from the fire that resulted from the earthquake.

Fires fed by broken gas pipes started in many of the damaged houses and buildings in the area south of Market Street. Since the water mains were broken, the fires spread rapidly, and in a few hours combined into a

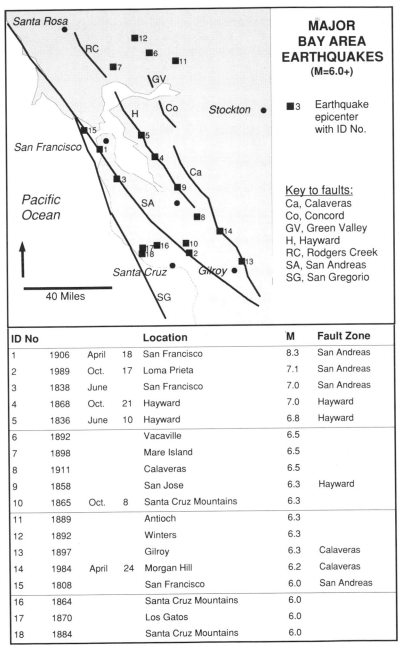

MAJOR BAY AREA EARTHQUAKES (M=6.0+)

■3 Earthquake epicenter with ID No.

Key to faults:
Ca, Calaveras
Co, Concord
GV, Green Valley
H, Hayward
RC, Rodgers Creek
SA, San Andreas
SG, San Gregorio

40 Miles

ID No				Location	M	Fault Zone
1	1906	April	18	San Francisco	8.3	San Andreas
2	1989	Oct.	17	Loma Prieta	7.1	San Andreas
3	1838	June		San Francisco	7.0	San Andreas
4	1868	Oct.	21	Hayward	7.0	Hayward
5	1836	June	10	Hayward	6.8	Hayward
6	1892			Vacaville	6.5	
7	1898			Mare Island	6.5	
8	1911			Calaveras	6.5	
9	1858			San Jose	6.3	Hayward
10	1865	Oct.	8	Santa Cruz Mountains	6.3	
11	1889			Antioch	6.3	
12	1892			Winters	6.3	
13	1897			Gilroy	6.3	Calaveras
14	1984	April	24	Morgan Hill	6.2	Calaveras
15	1808			San Francisco	6.0	San Andreas
16	1864			Santa Cruz Mountains	6.0	
17	1870			Los Gatos	6.0	
18	1884			Santa Cruz Mountains	6.0	

Since the early 1800's there have been eighteen earthquakes of M6.0 or greater in the Bay Area. Half of these earthquakes were on the San Andreas, Hayward and Calaveras faults.

single gigantic inferno that crept westwards across the city. By two days after the earthquake the fire had consumed much of North Beach and Chinatown. On the third day after the earthquake, the fires were fought back and extinguished, thanks to the help of wide Van Ness Avenue which provided a good firebreak.

Loma Prieta Earthquake: If you were in San Francisco at 5:04 PM on October 17, 1989, or watching the World Series on television at that time, you had a grandstand seat to the Loma Prieta Earthquake. The earthquake was strongly felt over much of the Bay Area south through Santa Cruz to Watsonville. Within this area the earthquake caused 67 deaths and $7.5 billion in damage to buildings, homes and other structures.

The earthquake was centered in the Santa Cruz Mountains, 56 miles south of San Francisco, and measured M7.1 on the Richter scale. Although this was not a "great" earthquake, it was substantial, and served as a wake-up call to San Francisco that the San Andreas fault is nearby. It also provided seismologists, city planners, architects, and engineers with a great deal of detailed data about how earthquakes form and how structures act during earthquakes.

The Loma Prieta Earthquake was caused by rupture of the rocks along the San Andreas fault. The epicenter of the earthquake was ten miles northwest of Santa Cruz, where the San Andreas fault makes a small jog to the west. Jogs such as this tend to hinder movement between the plates so that stresses can easily accumulate and cause larger earthquakes. This section of the San Andreas fault had only minor displacement in the 1906 earthquake, so that all of the pent-up stress may not have been released in 1906. Seismologists had therefore predicted that this section of the fault was ripe for a major earthquake.

The P waves from the earthquake reached Santa Cruz about three seconds after the rupture, and San Francisco about 16 seconds after the rupture. The S waves arrived in San Francisco ten seconds after the P waves. The earthquake waves were recorded on seismograms at 18 seismic stations throughout the world. The seismograms showed that the Loma Prieta Earthquake was located at N. Lat. 37° 2', W. Long. 121° 53', at a depth of 11.5 miles on the San Andreas fault. The earthquake measured M7.1 on the Richter scale. Detailed studies of earthquake records indicated that the rocks on the southwest side of the rupture moved up 4.6 feet and northwest 6.5 feet relative to the northeast side of the fault.

The aftershocks defined the rupture surface of the Loma Prieta Earthquake in detail. They showed that the rupture surface was 31 miles long and from one to twelve miles deep. They also showed that the fault plane dipped $70°$ southwest and that the rupture did not reach the surface of the ground. The Santa Cruz Mountains were uplifted about 14 inches as a result of the earthquake. Early media reports of finding the rupture on the surface were in error. The reported ruptures were related to other surficial disturbances caused by the earthquake, such as landslides.

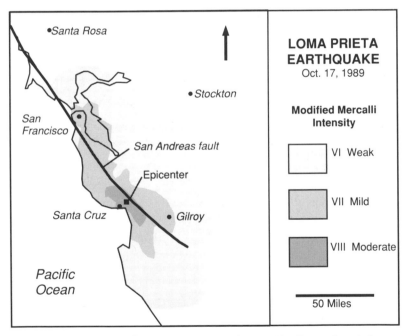

The epicenter of the M7.1 Loma Prieta Earthquake was 10 miles northeast of Santa Cruz and 56 miles south-southeast of San Francisco. Moderate shaking (MMI>VIII) occurred over an area about 25 miles by 10 miles, oriented along the San Andreas fault zone. Mild shaking (MMI>VII) occurred over an area of 100 miles by 20 miles, including much of San Francisco and the south Bay Area. Within the zone of moderate shaking there was strong and intense shaking in areas with unconsolidated sediments, such as the South of Market area in San Francisco.

Although the Loma Prieta Earthquake was felt over a broad area, the most severe damage was concentrated in a few local areas of loose unconsolidated sediments and in areas subject to liquefaction. Most of these severely damaged areas were in San Francisco, Oakland and Santa Cruz.

In San Francisco, heavily damaged areas included the Marina District, the South of Market area, the Embarcadero, and the Mission District. Throughout the city, 1,250 buildings were damaged to the extent that access was limited until repairs were made; 363 buildings were declared unsafe; and 22 buildings were damaged sufficiently to warrant demolition. In addition, major damage was done to several highway structures, including the Embarcadero Freeway and Highways 280 and 480. The parts of San Francisco built on hard rock were relatively unaffected by the earthquake.

The Marina District suffered from two major problems — liquefaction and poor building design. When liquefaction occurred in the loose sedimentary fill during the earthquake, building foundations had little lateral support, and the lower part of the buildings tended to spread laterally. Many of the buildings in the Marina District had parking garages on the lower floor and the open design of the garages offered little shear resistance to this lateral spreading. As a result, many buildings collapsed. Buildings in nearby areas that had been built on dune sand shook just as strongly during the earthquake, but suffered little damage, since there was no liquefaction.

In Oakland, the major damage was the collapse of a 1.5-mile section of I-880 known as the Cypress structure. This collapsed portion of the structure was built on thin bay mud and loose artificial fill. The portions of the structure that were built on older, harder alluvium did not fail.

Location	Rock Type	Peak Acceleration (g)	Peak Displacement (cm.)
Treasure Island	bay mud	.16	12.2
Telegraph Hill	hard rock	.08	2.8

Data from accelerograms recorded during the Loma Prieta Earthquake show that the acceleration and amount of movement of structures built on bay mud were considerably larger than for structures built on hard rock.

Earthquake Predictions

It is impossible at the present time to accurately predict the time, size and location of earthquakes. However, some generalizations can be made. In 1990, the U.S. Geological Survey estimated that there was a 67% probability that a M7.0 earthquake would occur in the Bay Area during the next 30 years. This estimate was based on studies of past earthquakes along the San Andreas, Hayward and Rodgers Creek faults. More recent studies show that a large earthquake may occur on several other faults in the Bay Area as well. Thus, the probability of a M7.0 earthquake will likely be increased to as much as 90%. Also, there are some indications that a future earthquake along the Hayward fault may be significantly larger than the M7.0 earthquake used in the planning studies, perhaps as large as M7.3 to M7.5. This new estimate is based on analysis of old survey data that shows that the break on the Hayward fault during the 1868 earthquake was larger than previously thought.

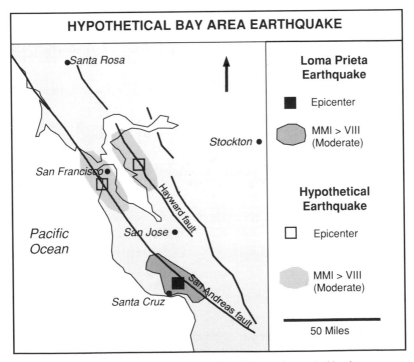

HYPOTHETICAL BAY AREA EARTHQUAKE

This map shows the areas that would be affected by moderate shaking by a hypothetical earthquake of the Loma Prieta size in the bay area.

ROCK TYPES, SAN FRANCISCO AREA

Igneous	Rocks crystallized from magma.	
Basalt	Black or dark green if fresh; most grains too small to see, but may have small white crystals of feldspar. Pillow basalt is basalt shaped like a stack of pillows.	Trip 2. Marin Headlands (Pt. Bonita Lighthouse)
Granite	Light gray, coarse grained, with large crystals of feldspar and quartz; weathers into blocks.	Trip 7. Pt. Reyes Peninsula (Sea Lion Overlook)
Serpentine	Green; slippery; heavy; waxy luster; breaks along curved surfaces, often with grooves.	Trip 1. San Francisco (Fort Point)
Ultramafic	Dark green or black; coarse grained; very heavy; composed of iron and magnesium silicate; mainly pyroxene and olivine.	Trip 4. Ring Mountain (Crest)
Sedimentary	**Rocks deposited in water, usually as grains of other rocks.**	
Sandstone	Sand grains cemented into a hard rock by deep burial; feels sandy.	Trip 5. Fort Funston (Bluff)
Graywacke	Similar to sandstone, but darker and has and fine-grained matrix of mud and silt.	Trip 1. San Francisco (Alcatraz,Cliff House)
Siltstone	Silt grains (too small too see); cemented into rock; feels gritty.	Trip 7. Pt. Reyes P. (Drakes Beach)
Shale	Mud or clay cemented into rock by deep burial; usually dark gray;soft; feels smooth; breaks into thin tablets.	Trip 7. Pt. Reyes P. (Agate Beach)
Chert	Smooth; very fine-grained; very hard; breaks into sharp fragments; occurs in red layers a few inches thick; silica-rich.	Trip 2. Marin Headlands (Battery 129)
Meta-morphic	**Sedimentary and igneous rocks altered by heat and/or pressure.**	
Schistose sandstone	Sandstone altered at moderate temperature and pressure; still has original sandstone texture; also has metamorphic minerals.	Trip 3. Angel Island (Ione Point)
Schist	Forms hard plates with shiny surfaces; original rock not obvious, may have been graywacke, basalt or other igneous rock. Blueschist has blue color from blue minerals that form at great depth and at abnormally low temperature.	Trip 3. Angel Island (Perle's Beach) (Camp Reynolds)
Exotic blocks	Large blocks in soft clay melange; blocks are strikingly different from the melange and other blocks in the melange.	Ring Mountain (Taylor Road)

ROCKS OF THE
SAN FRANCISCO AREA

Rock Types

The table on the opposite page briefly describes the various rocks that you will see on the geologic trips in the San Francisco area. There are three main types of rocks, *igneous, sedimentary and metamorphic*. Igneous rocks consist of minerals that have solidified or crystallized from molten rock, called magma. The crystals form as the magma cools, just as ice crystals form in a glass of water that is frozen. The type of igneous rock that is formed depends on the composition of the magma and the rate of cooling. If the magma cools slowly, large crystals are formed and the rock is coarse-grained, like the granite that you will see on the Point Reyes Peninsula. If the magma cools rapidly, the crystals are very small, usually too small to see without magnification, and the rock is fine-grained, like the basalt in the Marin Headlands.

When igneous rocks are subjected to erosion and weathering, they break into smaller fragments - pebbles, sand, silt, and clay. These *sediments* are carried by rivers to the ocean and deposited on the sea floor as sedimentary rocks. The most common sedimentary rocks are sandstone, graywacke, siltstone, and shale. You will see examples of these rocks on the trips to San Francisco, Fort Funston and the Marin Headlands. Some sedimentary rocks are also formed by precipitation of chemicals from supersaturated water. Chert forms from water supersaturated with silica. The red chert in the Marin Headlands was formed in this manner.

When igneous or sedimentary rocks are buried deeply in the earth by geologic processes, they are subjected to high heat and pressure and the rocks are altered, or *metamorphosed*. At very high temperatures and/or pressures new minerals are formed by alteration of the previous minerals, and the rock may take on a banded or platy appearance. Some rocks may be altered to the extent that they look quite different from the original rocks. You will see good examples of metamorphic rocks on the trips to Angel Island and Ring Mountain.

Franciscan Rocks

During the first four geologic trips in the San Francisco area you will see examples of many different types of Franciscan rocks - graywacke, shale, red chert, pillow basalt, serpentine, many types of metamorphic rocks, and thick units of melange. This unusual group of rocks was formed in the Franciscan subduction zone, mainly during Jurassic and Cretaceous time. The Franciscan rocks, although named for their excellent exposures in the San Francisco area, are widespread in the Coast Ranges of northern California. Patches of these rocks can be found in the Coast Ranges of Central California and as far south as Catalina Island offshore from Los Angeles.

The most common rock in the Franciscan is *graywacke*, a variety of sandstone that has a relatively small amount of quartz and a relatively high proportion of feldspar, rock fragments, and fine-grained matrix. The typical Franciscan graywacke is about 30% quartz, 30% feldspar, 25% grains of chert, volcanic rocks, metamorphic rocks, and/or shale, and 15% very fine-grained matrix. Graywacke usually occurs in beds that are a few inches to a few feet thick and is commonly interbedded with minor amounts of shale. The shale is similar in composition to the graywacke, but differs mainly in having smaller grain size.

Most Franciscan graywacke, like the graywacke in the Alcatraz terrane, contains *plagioclase* feldspar. This feldspar is rich in sodium and calcium, and was derived from rapid weathering of the volcanic-rich source areas that were prevalent during the early and middle phases of subduction. In contrast, the younger Franciscan graywackes, like the San Bruno Mountain terrane, often contain *K-feldspar*, which is rich in potassium. The K-feldspar was derived from weathering of granitic rocks in the ancient Sierras. This granite was not present during the early stages of subduction.

Melanges are quite common in the Franciscan of the Coast Ranges. The typical melange consists of soft blue-gray clay peppered with hard exotic blocks. Most Franciscan melanges are similar to the Tiburon, Hunters Point and City College melanges of the San Francisco area. The most extensive Franciscan melange is called the *Central Belt*, and lies north of San Francisco.

Volcanic rocks and greenstones make up about 10% of the Franciscan. These volcanic rocks include basalt flows, pillow basalts, agglomerates, tuffs, and diabase dikes, and are similar to the volcanic rocks of the Marin Headlands terrane. Chert is not common, but is fairly widespread, and is almost always associated with pillow basalt.

Most Franciscan rocks are not highly metamorphosed. The rocks that are metamorphosed generally fall into one of three distinct categories: extensive terranes, like the Angel Island terrane; small isolated patches of dense metamorphosed graywacke or greenstone; and metamorphosed exotic blocks that occur in the melanges, like the exotic blocks at Ring Mountain.

Serpentine is also widespread in the Franciscan. It can occur in thick sheets, like those at the top of Ring Mountain; as isolated blocks that have forced their way into other Franciscan rocks; or as blocks within melanges, like the serpentine blocks found in the Hunters Point melange at Fort Point.

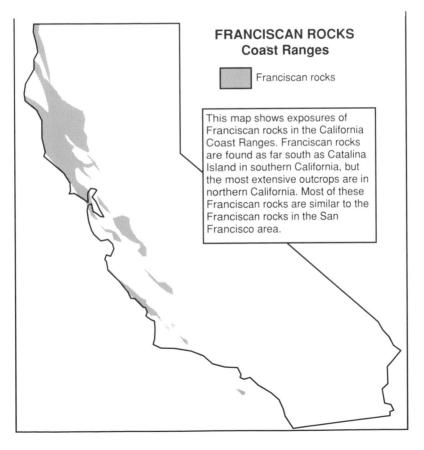

FRANCISCAN ROCKS
Coast Ranges

Franciscan rocks

This map shows exposures of Franciscan rocks in the California Coast Ranges. Franciscan rocks are found as far south as Catalina Island in southern California, but the most extensive outcrops are in northern California. Most of these Franciscan rocks are similar to the Franciscan rocks in the San Francisco area.

GEOLOGIC TIME SCALE				
Era	Period	Epoch	MY*	Event
Cenozoic	Quaternary	Holocene	0.01	Bluff formed, Fort Funston
		Pleistocene	2	Ice ages, early man (2 MY) San Francisco Bay formed Modern Coast Ranges formed Merced fm. deposited
	Tertiary	Pliocene	5	Drakes Bay fm. deposited Continued uplift of Coast Ranges
		Miocene	22	Monterey Shale deposited
		Oligocene	37	San Andreas fault formed (25 MY) Continued movement to present
		Eocene	58	Uplift and erosion of ancient Coast Ranges begins
		Paleocene	65	Pt. Reyes Conglomerate deposited
Mesozoic	Cretaceous	Upper	100	Last dinosaur (65 MY) Youngest Franciscan (65 MY) Franciscan subduction ends
		Lower	145	Granite intruded in Sierras
	Jurassic		208	Smartville docked Oldest Franciscan (175 MY)
	Triassic		245	Sonomia docked and North America extended to Sierras (225 MY) First dinosaur (275 MY)
Paleozoic			570	First fish (340 MY) First trilobite (570 MY)
Pre-Cambrian			4600	Bacteria (2100 MY) Formation of earth (4600 MY)

*MY - Millions of years to opening of time period

GEOLOGIC HISTORY
OF THE SAN FRANCISCO AREA

If you had visited San Francisco during early Jurassic time, 200 million years ago, you would not have seen much. You would have been in a deep ocean, an ancient version of the Pacific, and you would have been far from shore. The western edge of the North American plate was 100 miles to the east, near the present-day Sierra foothills. There was a subduction zone along the western boundary of the North American plate, near the present-day mother lode, and the oceanic plate under the ancient Pacific was moving east into that subduction zone.

If you had been patient and had stuck around until mid-Jurassic time, another 25 million years or so, you would have seen the Smartville terrane passing you by and headed toward this old subduction zone. Smartville was being carried toward the subduction zone on an ancient version of the Farallon plate. When the Smartville terrane reached the subduction zone, it plugged it up and became part of the North American plate. North America was thus extended to the present-day Coast Ranges. Since the old subduction zone was plugged up, a new subduction zone was formed along the new western margin of North America. The Farallon plate continued to move into this new *Franciscan* subduction zone, and the Franciscan rocks began to be formed.

For the next 110 million years, during late Jurassic and most of Cretaceous time, the ocean floor of the Farallon plate continued to move eastward into the Franciscan subduction zone. The lower part of the Farallon plate slid below the North American plate and was largely consumed in the earth's mantle. Much of the upper part of the plate was scraped off in the subduction zone to form the Franciscan rocks. Most of the new rock units that were added to the subduction zone were inserted below the rocks that were already in the subduction zone. Tens of thousands of feet of Franciscan rocks accumulated in the subduction zone in this manner, including the Angel Island terrane, the Alcatraz terrane, the Marin Headlands terrane, and the San Bruno Mountain terrane, as well as the melanges that separate these terranes.

Some of the Franciscan rocks were carried to depths of over 30 miles in the subduction zone. Other rocks were not buried very deeply, but were crumpled and rose above the surface of the ocean to form a chain of islands, an ancient version of the Coast Ranges.

While the Franciscan rocks accumulated in the subduction zone, magma was being generated at depth. This magma forced its way upward along the western edge of the North American plate. The magma cooled at depths of a few miles below the surface of the earth to form the granitic rocks of the Sierras. By late Cretaceous time many parts of the ancient Sierras were being uplifted and exposed to erosion. Some of the quartz and feldspar grains from the weathered granite were carried back into the subduction zone and became part of the younger Franciscan rocks, such as the San Bruno Mountain terrane.

By Oligocene time, the Farallon plate had been almost entirely consumed in the Franciscan subduction zone and the East Pacific Rise and Pacific plate began to enter the subduction zone. As the Pacific plate entered the subduction zone it was still moving northwest away from the East Pacific Rise spreading center. Since the Farallon plate was no longer pushing against the North American plate, subduction suddenly stopped. Instead, the Pacific plate captured the westernmost edge of the North American plate and began to carry it northwest with the rest of the Pacific plate. The San Andreas fault formed along this new boundary between the North American and Pacific plates, and the future Los Angeles began to slowly move north toward the future San Francisco.

Part of the large granite batholith that formed the southern Sierras was on the piece of the North American plate that was captured by the Pacific plate. This piece of granitic crust, now called the Salinian block, was carried several hundred miles to the north by the San Andreas fault. Parts of this block now form Montara Mountain and the basement rocks of the Point Reyes Peninsula.

During Tertiary time, the rocks along the old subduction zone began to be uplifted since they were no longer being pulled into the subduction zone. Eventually, they were uplifted high enough to form a range of mountains, an early form of the Coast Ranges. At times this range of mountains was separated from the Sierras by a shallow embayment of the ocean, an early form of the Great Valley. As uplift of the Coast Ranges continued, Franciscan rocks that had once been buried at depths of over 30 miles were eventually exposed at the surface of the earth.

Continuing movement along the San Andreas fault system broke the Coast Ranges into many large blocks. Some of these blocks continued to be uplifted whereas other subsided. Still others went up and then changed their minds and went down. The high blocks became mountain ranges. Sedimentary rocks were deposited in the low *basin* areas between the high blocks. Sedimentary rocks that accumulated in this manner include the Point Reyes Conglomerate during Paleocene time, the Monterey Shale during Miocene time, the Drakes Bay Formation during Pliocene time, and the Merced Formation during Pleistocene time. As the Coast Ranges continued to be jostled by the San Andreas fault, many of the sedimentary rocks in the basins were folded, faulted, and uplifted.

During Pliocene time, much of the Coast Ranges were eroded to a low, rolling topographic surface that was near sea level. In late Pliocene time, this nearly flat Pliocene topographic surface was broadly uplifted and began to be carved by rivers and the ocean. Most of the major topographic elements of the present Coast Ranges have been formed by erosion of this late Pliocene topographic surface. Remnants of this flattish erosional surface now form the tops of some of the mountains in the Coast Ranges, at elevations of several hundreds of feet to several thousands of feet. You are standing on this surface when you are at the top of Mt. Tamalpais, ten miles northwest of San Francisco.

Although most of the Coast Ranges continued to be uplifted during Pleistocene time, the area around San Francisco Bay subsided, and the Pacific Ocean reached eastward through the Golden Gate and flooded out to form San Francisco Bay. The hills near the Golden Gate were submerged to form the San Francisco peninsula, the Marin Headlands, and the Tiburon Peninsula. The tops of some of the hills became islands in the bay, such as Alcatraz Island and Angel Island.

During Pleistocene time, San Francisco Bay alternately emptied and filled as sea level fell and rose with the advances and retreats of the Pleistocene glaciers. When sea level was low, the Sacramento River flowed through the Golden Gate and deposited sand along the Pacific shoreline tens of miles west of the present shore. Much of this sand was blown inland to form the sand dunes that covered much of northern San Francisco. During interglacial times, as at present, sea level was high, the bay was full of water, and the Sacramento River dumped its load of sediments before reaching the bay.

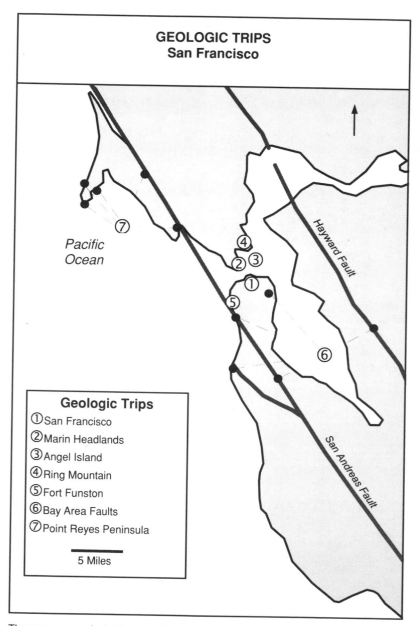

GEOLOGIC TRIPS
San Francisco

Pacific
Ocean

Hayward Fault

San Andreas Fault

Geologic Trips

① San Francisco
② Marin Headlands
③ Angel Island
④ Ring Mountain
⑤ Fort Funston
⑥ Bay Area Faults
⑦ Point Reyes Peninsula

5 Miles

These seven geologic trips provide a sampling of the rocks and geology of the Bay Area. Most of the trips can be easily done in one day, although two days should be allowed for the trip to the Point Reyes Peninsula.

PART II

THE GEOLOGIC TRIPS

GEOLOGIC TRIPS
Location: ● *Geologic site*

Trip 1. San Francisco
Alcatraz Island: ● *Officers Club,* ● *Cellblocks*
Fort Point: ● *Parking Lot,* ● *Baker Beach Bluff*
Palace of the Legion of Honor: ● *Landslide*
Cliff House: ● *Cliff House,* ● *Sutro Baths*
Twin Peaks: ● *Viewpoint*

Trip 2. Marin Headlands
Battery 129: ● *Parking Area*
Point Bonita Lighthouse: ● *Lighthouse*
Rodeo Beach: ● *North End,* ● *Rodeo Beach,* ● *South End*

Trip 3. Angel Island
Ione Point: ● *Perimeter Road*
Camp Reynolds: ● *Seawall,* ● *South End of Beach*
Perle's Beach: ● *East End,* ● *West End*
Rock Crusher: ● *Serpentine Quarry*
Fort McDowell: ● *Guard House*

Trip 4. Ring Mountain
Taylor Road: ● *Parking Area,* ● *Crest*

Trip 5. Fort Funston
Ocean Beach: ● *Beach*
Fort Funston: ● *Viewing Platform,* ● *Bluff*

Trip 6. Bay Area Faults
Mussel Rock: ● *Westline Drive,* ● *Longview Playground,* ● *Skyline Drive*
Devils Slide: ● *North End,* ● *Landslide,* ● *Gray Whale Cove*
Crystal Springs Reservoir: ● *Causeway,* ● *San Andreas Dam*
Hayward: ● *Mission Blvd.,* ● *D Street,* ● *Prospect Street*
South of Market: ● *Clara Street*

Trip 7. Point Reyes Peninsula
Bear Valley Visitor Center: ● *Earthquake Trail*
Point Reyes Headlands: ● *Sea Lion Overlook,* ● *Lighthouse*
South Beach: ● *South Beach*
Drakes Beach: ● *Drakes Beach*
Bolinas: ● *Bolinas Bluff,* ● *Agate Beach*

OVERVIEW OF THE TRIPS

The seven geologic trips listed on the opposite page have been selected to sample different aspects of the geology of the Coast Ranges in and around San Francisco. On the first four trips — to San Francisco, the Marin Headlands, Angel Island, and Ring Mountain — you will see examples of the many different types of Franciscan rocks that occur in the Bay Area. During Trip 5, to Fort Funston, you will see how some of the younger sedimentary rocks in the Bay Area were formed. On Trip 6 you will see the San Andreas and Hayward faults and how they have affected the landscape, buildings, and life in the Bay Area. Trip 7 is to the Point Reyes Peninsula where you will walk along the San Andreas fault and see rocks on the peninsula that have been abducted from southern and central California and carried northward tens to hundreds of miles by the fault.

During each trip you will visit a number of specific geologic sites to look at the rocks and geology in detail. Many of these sites are along the shoreline. It is best to go to the shoreline on a calm day and at low tide, preferably in winter when the rocks are clean and bare. Be on the lookout for sneaker waves and watch your step where rocks are slippery.

Use caution and common sense while on the geologic trips. Drive, park and hike safely. Do not go along the seashore if conditions are potentially dangerous, and do not go anywhere that you feel may be unsafe. On inland trails try to avoid the ubiquitous poison oak. Changes by man or nature can occur along any of the roads, hiking trails, and especially along the shoreline.

Collecting rocks is prohibited on Angel Island, in the Golden Gate National Recreation Area, and in the Point Reyes National Seashore. In other areas it is best not to collect the rocks unless you have received permission or know that collecting is permitted. To see the details of the rocks, bring a hand lens or magnifying glass if you have one. You may be surprised at what you see.

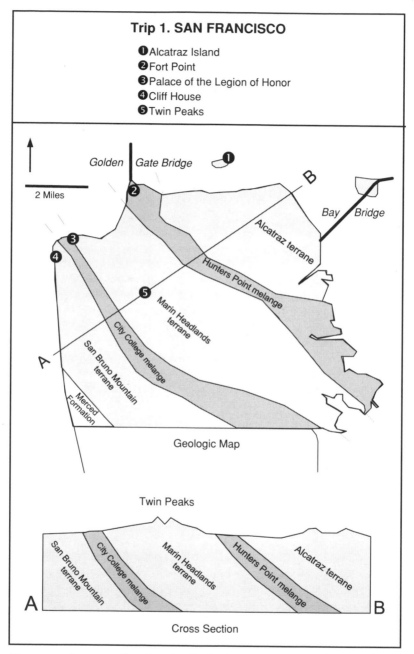

Trip 1. SAN FRANCISCO

❶ Alcatraz Island
❷ Fort Point
❸ Palace of the Legion of Honor
❹ Cliff House
❺ Twin Peaks

Golden Gate Bridge

2 Miles

Bay Bridge

Alcatraz terrane

Hunters Point melange

Marin Headlands terrane

City College melange

San Bruno Mountain terrane

Merced Formation

Geologic Map

Twin Peaks

San Bruno Mountain terrane

City College melange

Marin Headlands terrane

Hunters Point melange

Alcatraz terrane

A

B

Cross Section

The map and cross section show the distribution of the five major Franciscan rock units that underlie San Francisco. Examples of each of these rock units will be seen during the geologic trip to San Francisco.

Trip 1.
SAN FRANCISCO
The Franciscan

San Francisco rests on a foundation of Franciscan rocks. Although there are many different types of Franciscan rocks, they share a common parentage in that they were all brought together in the Franciscan subduction zone during the collision between the Farallon plate and the North American plate in Jurassic and Cretaceous time from 65 to 175 million years ago.

The Franciscan rocks in San Francisco have been divided by geologists into five different rock units. You will see examples of each of these rock units during this geologic trip to San Francisco. The trip can be easily completed by car in one day. These are the places you will visit:

<u>Alcatraz Island:</u> Alcatraz Island is made up of thick sandstones of the Alcatraz terrane. At Alcatraz you will learn where these sandstones came from and why they got sentenced to Alcatraz for life.

<u>Fort Point:</u> The fort at Fort Point is built on a large block of serpentine within the Hunters Point melange. This serpentine is a piece of oceanic crust from the lower part of the Farallon plate.

<u>Palace of the Legion of Honor:</u> Here you will see a landslide that was responsible for closing a half-mile section of El Camino del Mar. The landslide was caused by the weak rocks of the City College melange.

<u>Cliff House:</u> Cliff House is built on thick sandstone beds of the San Bruno Mountain terrane. These sandstones were deposited in a deep oceanic trough along the Franciscan subduction zone during upper Cretaceous time.

<u>Twin Peaks:</u> The Twin Peaks consist of pillow basalt and red chert of the Marin Headlands terrane. These rocks once formed the upper part of the Farallon plate when the Farallon plate was several thousand miles west of San Francisco.

The Franciscan rocks in San Francisco occur in five northwest-trending bands that cut diagonally across the city. If you were to trace these rocks deep below the earth's surface, you would find that the rocks form layers that are stacked like giant pancakes on a platter tilted to the northeast. The bands of rocks that you see on the surface are the uptilted edges of these rock layers.

This is not an ordinary platter of pancakes. In this stack, the oldest layer, the Alcatraz terrane, is on the top of the stack and the youngest layer, the San Bruno Mountain terrane, is on the bottom. The younger rock units were stuffed under the older rock units as the rock units entered the Franciscan subduction zone. It's as if the younger pancakes were stuffed under the older pancakes on the platter.

After the subduction was completed, the Franciscan rocks were uplifted and eroded. Rocks that had once been buried at depths of up to 30 miles in the subduction zone were eventually exposed at the surface of the ground. These rocks now make up the hills of San Francisco and many of the islands in the bay.

FRANCISCAN ROCKS San Francisco			
Locality	Rock Unit	Age	Description
Alcatraz Island	Alcatraz terrane	Lower Cretaceous	Graywacke sandstone, little or no K-feldspar
Fort Point	Hunters Point melange	Jurassic Cretaceous	Melange: large blocks of serpentine in soft clay and serpentine matrix
Twin Peaks	Marin Headlands terrane	Jurassic Cretaceous	Pillow basalt, red chert and sandstone, typically in thin fault slices
Palace of the Legion of Honor	City College melange	Jurassic Cretaceous	Melange: blocks of basalt, chert, and sandstone in soft clay and serpentine matrix
Cliff House	San Bruno Mountain terrane	Upper Cretaceous	Graywacke sandstone, contains K-feldspar

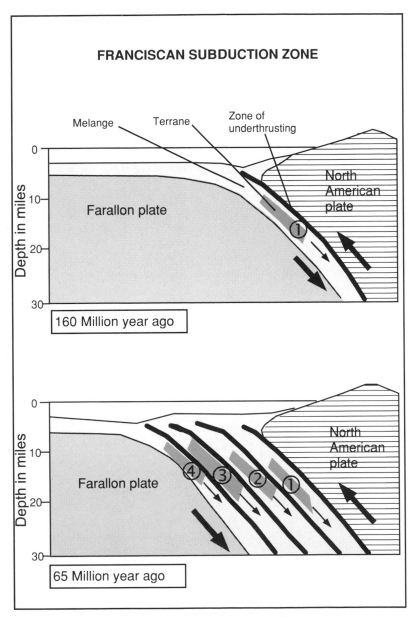

In this model of the Franciscan subduction zone, terrane ① went into the subduction zone first, followed by terranes②, ③, and ④. These terranes entered the subduction zone during Jurassic and Cretaceous time. At the end of the Cretaceous, the rocks in the subduction zone were uplifted. Eventually, rocks that had been buried at depths of 30 miles were exposed at the surface by erosion of the overlying rocks.

Alcatraz Island

Alcatraz Island is the best place in the Bay Area to see the Alcatraz terrane of the Franciscan. The Alcatraz terrane is characterized by thick-bedded sandstones. These sandstones form many of the hills that give downtown San Francisco its unique character, including Telegraph Hill, Russian Hill, Rincon Hill and Nob Hill. However, in San Francisco, the Alcatraz sandstone is almost everywhere covered by buildings, streets and cable car tracks, so that good exposures are hard to find.

All of the rocks that you see on Alcatraz Island belong to the Alcatraz terrane. There are numerous good exposures of these rocks, but access is limited by the Park Service and the sea gulls. The trick is to find outcrops of the Alcatraz sandstones that are accessible. Two geologic sites will be described on this trip, the Officers Club and the Cellblocks. Along the path near the Officers Club you will examine the sandstone in detail and learn where the sand grains came from. At the Cellblocks you will see the thick and massive character of the sandstone beds that has made them so resistant to erosion.

To get to Alcatraz Island, take a Red and White Ferry from Pier 41 at Fisherman's Wharf (Phone 1-800-BAY CRUISE). Departures are at 30-minute intervals throughout the day and tickets go on sale at 8 AM. During the summer you should make advance reservations.

In the late 1800's and early 1900's, Alcatraz Island was controlled by the U.S. Army, which used it as a fort and later as a military prison. The federal government took control in 1934 and used it until 1963 as a high-security penitentiary for criminals considered too dangerous to be held in conventional jails. In 1972 Alcatraz became part of the Golden Gate National Recreation Area. The GGNRA now provides an excellent self-guided tour of the penitentiary, and you should go on this tour while you are on "The Rock."

During the glacial stages of the Pleistocene, when sea level was exceptionally low, there was no water in San Francisco Bay and Alcatraz Island was connected by land to San Francisco. Alcatraz at these times was just another hill like Telegraph Hill, Nob Hill, Russian Hill, and Rincon Hill. During these periods of low sea level, the Sacramento River flowed westward through Raccoon Strait between Angel Island and the Tiburon Peninsula and then through the Golden Gate. There is still a deep channel in the bay through Raccoon Strait that follows this old river channel.

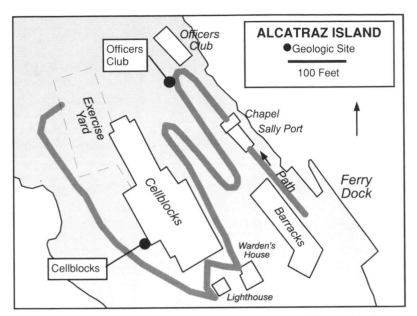

Alcatraz Island consists of sandstones of the Alcatraz terrane. These rocks form many of the hills in downtown San Francisco, but the best exposures are on Alcatraz Island.

The steep cliffs on the southwest shore of Alcatraz Island are formed from thick beds of the Alcatraz sandstone.

●Officers Club

Follow the path from the ferry dock past the Sally Port and Chapel to the first switchback at the Officers Club. At this switchback you will see outcrops of the Alcatraz sandstone in the cuts along the path. If you look at the sandstone in detail you will see that it forms layers a foot or so thick and that these layers dip steeply to the east. The sandstone is light yellow-brown in color and feels like sandpaper when you rub it. If you examine the sandstone with a magnifying glass, you will see that it is composed of many small grains that are cemented together. It's like beach sand, only much harder. Most of the grains are about the size of a pinhead and are sharp and angular. Under a microscope, you would see that there are several different types of sand grains. Most of the grains are milky, opaque feldspar. About a third of the grains are clear, glassy quartz. The other grains include shale, volcanic rocks, metamorphic rocks, and red chert. The spaces between the sand grains are filled with clay and very small grains of other minerals and rocks.

The sand grains were derived from the many different types of rocks that were being eroded along the margin of the North American continent during early Cretaceous time. These rocks were broken into small sand grains by weathering and erosion. The sand grains were then carried by rivers to the ocean and deposited on the sea floor. The transportation and deposition of the sand grains took place rapidly. The sand grains would have been rounded if transportation had been for long distances. Also, the grains composed of soft volcanic rocks and shale would not have survived long transportation. The clay, mica, and chlorite that make up the matrix of the sandstone are mainly weathering products formed by chemical alteration of the less resistant rocks in the source area. Dirty sandstones such as these are referred to by geologists as graywackes. Most of the sandstones in the Franciscan are graywackes.

●Cellblocks

To get to this locality, follow the path to the west side of the island, where you can see the west side of the Cellblocks. The Cellblocks are built on very thick beds of Alcatraz sandstone. These thick sandstone beds form the steep cliffs on this side of the island. Note that the sandstones exposed in these cliffs form layers about 10 to 20 feet thick. When the sandstone was deposited on the sea floor during Lower Cretaceous time, it was deposited one layer at a time, each layer covering the previous layer on the sea floor. These layers of sand were horizontal when they were originally deposited. The tilting occurred during subsequent uplift and folding of the rocks. Probably most of the tilting occurred when the Alcatraz sandstone was carried into the

Franciscan subduction zone a few million years after it was deposited. Where these layers are especially thick, they are very resistant to weathering and erosion. These thick sandstones have given us many of the hills in downtown San Francisco.

The wall at the right is part of the Exercise Yard at Alcatraz. This wall is built on massive sandstone cliffs of the Alcatraz terrane in the center of the photo.

Telegraph Hill: If it is not convenient to get to Alcatraz Island, you can also see some exposures of the Alcatraz sandstone at Telegraph Hill. To do this, go to Sansome and Union Street on the east side of Telegraph Hill. On the west side of this intersection you will see a large cliff of Alcatraz sandstone. Years back, this cliff was the face of a rock quarry. The sandstone in the cliff is very massive; that is, it is not interbedded with soft shale beds. It is because this sandstone is so massive that Telegraph Hill has resisted weathering and erosion.

You can see other exposures of the sandstone along the pathway to Coit Tower that leaves from the intersection of Lombard Street and Telegraph Hill Blvd. Do not be fooled by the large red boulders along the road at the top of Coit Tower. These rocks are jasper, and were carried here by truck from somewhere else.

Fort Point

The point of land that guards the south side of the Golden Gate is a large block of serpentine that lies within the Hunters Point melange of the Franciscan. The fort at Fort Point was built on this block of serpentine. Another large block of serpentine supports the south tower of the Golden Gate Bridge. The Hunters Point melange contains a number of these large blocks of serpentine. During the trip to Fort Point you will visit the parking lot at Fort Point and the bluff at Baker Beach. At the parking lot you will see part of the serpentine block that underlies the fort and at the Baker Beach bluff you will see the Hunters Point melange where it contains smaller blocks of serpentine and many other rocks.

To get to Fort Point from Fisherman's Wharf, go west on Bay Street to Van Ness Ave., turn left and go three blocks to Lombard Street, turn right and go 1.2 miles to Lincoln Blvd. Turn right on Lincoln Blvd. then right on Long Ave. Follow Long Ave. and Marine Drive to the parking area at Fort Point. Fort Point National Historic Site is within the Golden Gate National Recreation Area. The fort is open daily 10 AM to 5 PM. For information, phone 415-556-1693.

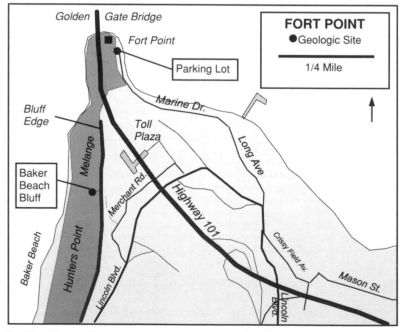

Fort Point was built on a large block of serpentine that lies within the Hunters Point melange of the Franciscan.

●*Parking Lot*

The large serpentine block that forms the foundation for the fort is exposed in the small hill at the parking lot next to the fort. The serpentine in this exposure is light green, flaky, and intensely foliated with many curved surfaces along which the serpentine tends to break. The foliations wrap around smaller blocks of hard serpentine that are darker green. The serpentine feels very slippery and has a waxy luster. Some of the dark green blocks appear as if they have been polished. There are other good exposures of this serpentine in the road cuts all along Marine Drive.

Serpentine is formed at spreading centers. It consists of ultramafic rocks from the earth's mantle that were altered by hot seawater. The hot seawater reached the ultramafic rocks through cracks formed in the earth's crust during the spreading process. The serpentine was carried away from the spreading center as the oceanic plate moved away from the spreading center. Serpentine forms the lower part of the earth's oceanic crust worldwide.

Fort Point, which lies under the south approach to the Golden Gate Bridge, is framed by a special arch on the bridge that was built to preserve the fort. The serpentine of the Hunters Point melange is exposed in the small hill at the parking lot to the left of the fort.

Serpentine is very common in the Franciscan throughout the Coast Ranges. In some places the serpentine occurs as small, isolated blocks and in other places as mountain-sized slabs. The most extensive exposures of serpentine are along the eastern edge of the northern Coast Ranges where a large slab from one- to five-miles wide and 70 miles long separates the Franciscan from the sedimentary rocks that were deposited in the Great Valley. The sedimentary rocks in the Great Valley were apparently deposited on this oceanic crust, then the Franciscan was thrust under this oceanic crust during subduction.

Many of the smaller isolated blocks of serpentine in the Franciscan represent pieces of the oceanic crust that were broken up and then squeezed upward through the overlying host rock like watermelon seeds. The serpentine in these blocks tends to break into small, dark green fragments with curved polished surfaces. The polished surfaces have tiny grooves that formed when the fragments rubbed against each other as the serpentine was squeezed through the rocks. Wherever you see serpentine on land, you are looking at a piece of oceanic crust that is out of place and was somehow injected into or squeezed onto the land.

This photo shows the bluff at the north end of Baker Beach. The rocks in the foreground are blocks of serpentine in the Hunters Point melange. The large rocks in the surf zone have been excavated from the Hunters Point melange by the waves at the base of the bluff.

● *Baker Beach Bluff*

To get to the bluff at Baker Beach from Fort Point, return on Long Ave. to Lincoln Blvd., turn right on Lincoln Blvd., and then take the road that goes to the Toll Plaza. Follow this road under the Toll Plaza to Merchant Road and park in the large parking area on Merchant Road Take the path to the Coastal Trail, then follow the trail north until you go down a short wooden staircase. At the base of the stairs leave the Coastal Trail and follow the path to the edge of the bluff.

The bluff here is made up of the Hunters Point melange. The melange consists of finely crushed serpentine, shale and sandstone with large random blocks of serpentine and many other rocks. There are many landslide deposits along the bluff and it is difficult in some places to distinguish between the landslides and the melange. Along the shoreline are numerous large boulders that have accumulated after being eroded from the melange. These boulders include sandstone and shale, basalt, chert, greenstone, serpentine polished by wave action, serpentine with small veins of asbestos, red jasper, yellow jasper, intensely deformed sandstone cemented by quartz and calcite veins, and metamorphosed gabbro. Since this beach is somewhat secluded, on a sunny day you may see much more exposed than just these rocks.

The Hunters Point melange occurs in a wide belt that trends southeast through San Francisco from Fort Point to Hunters Point. Because the clay in the melange is soft, there are few exposures of the clay along the outcrop belt. However, the large serpentine blocks within the melange are hard and therefore typically form small hills along the outcrop belt.

During construction of the Golden Gate Bridge there was some controversy concerning whether the serpentine block under the south tower would provide adequate support for the bridge. To settle this dispute, Andy Lawson, who was then a Professor of Geology at U.C. Berkeley, was lowered into the deep foundation hole that had been dug into the serpentine. Professor Lawson proclaimed that the rock was satisfactory and construction of the bridge continued. Another large block of serpentine forms the foundation of the New Mint building at Dubose and Church Streets. The mint building is built on a small hill, and the serpentine can be seen directly under the mint building. This is probably the best exposure of serpentine in San Francisco. The serpentine under the mint consists of blocks of serpentine a couple of feet in diameter that are surrounded by highly foliated serpentine. Other large blocks of serpentine form Portrero Hill and Hunters Point.

Palace of the Legion of Honor

Some years back you could drive west along El Camino del Mar from the Palace of the Legion of Honor to Ocean Lookout Park. This section of El Camino del Mar was built on the City College melange of the Franciscan and is now abandoned because of landslides caused by the weak and slippery clay in the melange. During the geologic trip to the Palace of the Legion of Honor you will visit one of these landslides.

To get to the Palace of the Legion of Honor from Fort Point, go west on Lincoln Blvd. to El Camino del Mar, and follow El Camino del Mar to Legion of Honor Drive. Do not turn left on Legion of Honor Drive, but continue west on El Camino del Mar about 200 yards until you reach the barrier across El Camino del Mar. This section of the road is now used as a parking area. Park here and go the road barrier.

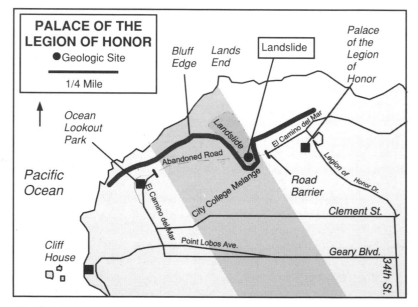

The City College melange consists of soft clay that contains hard blocks of basalt, serpentine, sandstone and other rocks. The soft clay in the melange has caused landslides that have led to abandonment of a half-mile section of El Camino del Mar.

●*Landslide*

To get to the landslide, take the path going west from the road barrier at the end of El Camino del Mar. Immediately past the barrier, the path goes down a 100 or so steps and then crosses a small bridge. The steps are on the landslide and the bridge is in a gully that was formed by the landslide. Near the bridge there are large chunks of asphalt from the abandoned road, and just beyond the bridge there is a large section of asphalt with the white mid-line stripe still on the asphalt. These pieces of the roadway have slid downslope about 50 feet courtesy of the landslide.

If you have the time, continue west on the abandoned section of the road. By keeping track of the pieces of asphalt you can see where several sections of the road are missing. In less than half a mile you will reach the road barrier at Ocean Lookout Park, where El Camino del Mar continues to the west. While at Ocean Lookout Park you can see the memorial to the U.S.S. San Francisco, which was lost during the battle of Guadacanal. Just north of the memorial you will find some wooden steps that go down to the Coastal Trail. Go down these steps, then along the Coastal Trail a few feet to the east to where you can get a view along the

This barrier marks the end of El Camino del Mar west of the Palace of the Legion of Honor. This section of the roadway was removed by a landslide in the soft rocks of the City College melange. The steps in the photo lead down the landslide. The continuation of the road can be seen on the other side of the gully.

bluff to the east toward Lands End. Be careful and don't go on the bluff where it is unsafe.

Most of the rocks exposed along the bluff between Ocean Lookout Park and Lands End are the City College melange. The melange consists of hard blocks of serpentine, schist, gabbro, basalt, chert, and sandstone in a soft matrix of fine clay and serpentine. As this section of the bluff has been eroded by the ocean waves, the hard boulders in the melange have remained behind and accumulated at the base of the bluff. These boulders now protect the bluff from rapid erosion.

In the early 1880's, a rail line had followed this same route and took people from downtown San Francisco to the Cliff House. The rail line was abandoned at the turn of the century because of maintenance problems related to the unstable roadbed. The fine clay matrix of the melange tends to hold the water near the surface and therefore becomes very slippery when wet. The clay then flows downhill, taking with it the roads, buildings, and whatever else has been built on the melange.

The clay matrix in the melange provides weak and slippery rocks wherever exposed in San Francisco. The rocks along the bluff are especially susceptible to landslides because the rocks are on a very steep slope. This combination of weak rocks, steep slope and heavy rainfall conspired to do away with this section of El Camino del Mar.

The City College melange cuts across San Francisco from Lands End through Golden Gate Park and McLaren Park to San Francisco Bay just south of Candlestick Park. The melange was formed along the zone of thrusting between the rocks of the San Bruno Mountain terrane and the Marin Headlands terrane while the rocks were in the Franciscan subduction zone. The fine clay matrix of the melange was formed from rocks that were thoroughly ground up by the thrusting. The blocks in the melange are pieces of hard rock that survived the grinding.

Melanges are very common in the Franciscan throughout the Coast Ranges of Northern California. Large random boulders on rolling hillsides are a tip-off that the rocks may be a melange. The boulders are very hard and stand out from the soft greenish-gray or bluish-gray clay matrix, which is seldom seen. The clay matrix does not have the thin layering of typical Franciscan shale. Landslides are especially common where the melange occurs on a steep slope.

These steps just beyond the barrier near the Palace of the Legion of Honor go down the landslide that took out a several-hundred-foot section of El Camino del Mar. Pieces of the old road surface can be seen in the landslide debris near the base of the steps.

The lump of asphalt in the center of this photo is one of many pieces of El Camino del Mar that can be found in the landslide debris just below the steps in the above photo. Note the white midline stripe above and to the right of the hat.

Cliff House

The sandstones of the San Bruno Mountain terrane were deposited as a series of submarine fans that filled a deepwater trough that had formed along the Franciscan subduction zone during late Cretaceous time. At the Cliff House and nearby Sutro Baths you will see some of these deepwater sandstones. The Cliff House was built on thick sandstone beds that had been deposited in the central parts of one of the submarine fans. The Sutro Baths are located in thinly bedded sandstone and shale that had been deposited along the edges of the fan.

To get to the Cliff House from the Palace of the Legion of Honor, follow Legion of Honor Drive to Geary Blvd. and turn right. Follow Geary Blvd. to Fortieth Avenue and then continue on Point Lobos Ave. to the Cliff House. Since the 1850's the Cliff House and its predecessors, including the Ocean House and Seal Rock House saloons, have been prime tourist destinations. The Cliff House is in the Golden Gate National Recreation Area. For information from the Park Service, phone 415-556-8642.

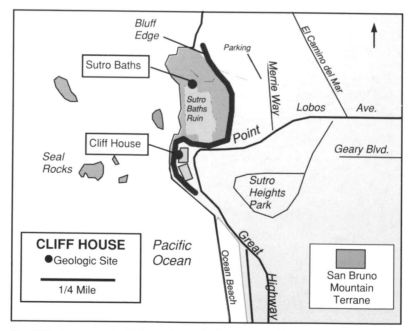

The Cliff House and the Sutro Baths are built on sandstones of the San Bruno Mountain terrane of the Franciscan.

● *Cliff House*

To see the thick sandstones of the San Bruno Mountain terrane, go down the steps leading to the visitor center on the observation deck at the Cliff House. The sandstone beds are exposed in the cliff below the observation deck. Continue south along the deck to where some of the sandstone is exposed along the path. The sandstone is light yellow brown, and the beds are very thick. There are almost no layers of black shale between the sandstone beds. The sandstone appears similar to the massive sandstone below the cellblocks at Alcatraz. However, there are a couple of differences. The sandstones of the San Bruno Mountain terrane are younger than the sandstones of the Alcatraz terrane. They were formed in late Cretaceous time during the later stages of subduction, whereas the rocks in the Alcatraz terrane were formed in early Cretaceous time during the earlier stages of subduction. Also, the sandstone in the San Bruno Mountain terrane contains K-feldspar, a variety of feldspar that is rich in potassium. The K-feldspar was derived from weathering of granitic rocks in the ancestral Sierras. These granitic rocks had been formed in the Franciscan subduction zone. There is almost no K-feldspar in the sandstones of the Alcatraz terrane since the Alcatraz sandstones were formed in the early stages of subduction before the Sierra granite had been subjected to erosion.

The massive sandstones under the Cliff House, like those at Alcatraz Island, are highly resistant to erosion.

●Sutro Baths

The Sutro Baths were built by Adolph Sutro, a popular San Francisco philanthropist. The indoor bathhouse was opened in 1896 and had seven separate pools spread across a three-acre site. The baths were enormously popular into the 1920's, but declined thereafter, and were destroyed in a fire in 1966.

The ruins of the Sutro Baths lie immediately north of the Cliff House. To get to the ruins from the Cliff House, go east on Point Lobos Ave. one block to Merrie Way, turn left, and park in the parking area. Take the path that leads to the tunnel immediately north of the ruins. At the entrance to this tunnel there are good exposures of interbedded sandstone and shale of the San Bruno Mountain terrane. The sandstone beds are similar to the sandstone at the Cliff House except that the beds are thinner, from one- to ten-feet thick. The hard sandstones form ridges that stick out from the soft black shale that occurs between the sandstone beds. Because the sandstone beds here are thin and interbedded with the soft shale, they are eroded more easily than the massive sandstone under the Cliff House. The cliff thus makes a reentrant in these softer rocks.

The sandstone that makes up the San Bruno Mountain terrane extends southeast from Cliff House through San Bruno Mountain to Oyster Cove on San Francisco Bay. There are extensive exposures of the sandstone in San Bruno Mountain State Park and San Bruno Mountain County Park.

From studies of sandstones in many other parts of the world, we know that the sandstones in the San Bruno Mountain terrane were deposited in deep ocean water by *turbidity currents*, dense mixtures of water and sediments that flow down the slope of the sea floor like underwater avalanches. A huge amount of sand and other sediments was required to form the widespread sandstones of the San Bruno Mountain terrane.

Most of the sediments that make up the San Bruno Mountain terrane were derived from the weathering and erosion of granitic rocks of the ancestral Sierras. These sediments were carried westward from the Sierras by ancient rivers to the ocean, and then carried along the coast until they reached a submarine canyon. The sediments accumulated on the sea floor near the head of the submarine canyon until they became unstable, perhaps because of a violent storm or earthquake. When the sediments became unstable, they slumped, mixed with ocean water, and formed a turbidity current. Since the turbidity current was heavier than

The Sutro Baths lie in a reentrant along the cliff just north of the Cliff House. Here, the sandstones in the San Bruno Mountain terrane are interbedded with many layers of soft black shale. This reentrant in the cliff was formed because these rocks are more easily eroded than the thick massive sandstones that form the cliff under the Cliff House.

the ocean water, it flowed down the submarine canyon until it reached the base of the canyon. At the base of the canyon the turbidity current would spread out onto a large fan in deep water and the sand and mud were deposited on the surface of the fan. The sand settled out of the turbidity current rapidly, and the fine mud settled out slowly at the end of the flow.

Each turbidity current flow typically resulted in deposition of a flat layer, or "bed" of sediments, with sand at the base and mud at the top. Over time, many beds of sand and mud accumulated on the fan in this manner, one on top of the other, eventually forming a unit of sandstone and mud several thousand feet thick and covering several hundred square miles. The mud is now represented by the layers of shale that occur between the sandstones.

Twin Peaks

San Francisco's famous Twin Peaks are formed from red chert and pillow basalt of the Marin Headlands terrane of the Franciscan. On this trip you will park at the viewpoint at the top of Twin Peaks and then take a short walk along the loop road to see these rocks.

To reach the Twin Peaks viewpoint from the Cliff House, go south on the Great Highway to Sloat Blvd., turn left and follow Sloat Blvd. to Portola Drive. Follow Portola Drive to Twin Peaks Blvd., and then continue on Twin Peaks Blvd. to the parking area for the viewpoint. The viewpoint is in Twin Peaks Park, and provides an excellent view of San Francisco, looking directly down Market Street to San Francisco Bay.

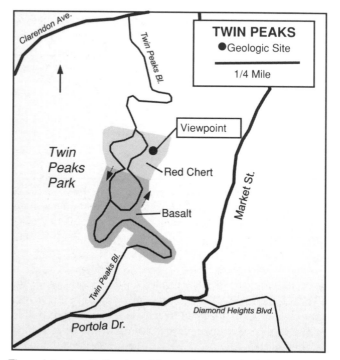

The red chert and pillow basalt that make up much of the Marin Headlands terrane are well exposed along the loop road at the top of Twin Peaks. The northern peak consists of red chert and the southern peak is pillow basalt.

● *Viewpoint*

Upon arriving at the viewpoint, be different from everyone else. Instead of going to the observation area to look at the city, take a walk on the one-way road that circles the two peaks. On this walk you will see that the Twin Peaks are not identical twins, but fraternal twins. The southern peak consists of pillow basalt and the northern peak consists of red chert.

If you start from the parking area for the viewpoint on the northern peak and follow the loop counterclockwise, you will first see the red chert in the road cuts. The red chert appears as bands about one- to two-inches thick. The chert is very hard and will scratch a knife blade or glass. The hard, red chert resists weathering and therefore tends to form ridges and hill tops. As you continue on the loop you will see that the road cuts in the southern peak are quite different. They consist of pillow basalt, which on these weathered exposures looks chunky and yellow-brown.

The red chert and the pillow basalt were formed along the East Pacific Rise spreading center during Jurassic time when the spreading center was far west of the North American continent. As the rocks were formed, they became the upper part of the Farallon plate and were carried hundreds of miles eastward into the Franciscan subduction zone. You will see these same rocks on the trip to the Marin Headlands and learn in more detail how the red chert and pillow basalt were formed.

As you leave the Twin Peaks, return to San Francisco by taking Twin Peaks Blvd. to the north. Along this road you will see many more exposures of the red chert that forms the northern peak.

The rocks of the Marin Headlands terrane extend as a broad band from Baker Beach through the eastern part of Golden Gate Park to Candlestick Hill. This band of rocks includes several hills that are formed primarily from the red chert, including Mt. Sutro, Diamond Heights, Bernal Heights, Mt. Davidson, and Candlestick Hill. These hills formed where the chert was especially thick. In other areas along the outcrop belt, where the red chert in more poorly developed, the Marin Headlands terrane occurs as small random exposures of pillow basalt, red chert and sandstone. These rocks can be seen at Billy Goat Hill near Diamond Heights, the Corona Heights Playground, and Glen Canyon Park. At Billy Goat Hill, the pillows in the pillow basalt form a short staircase up the side of the hill.

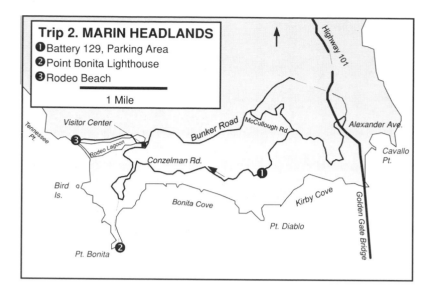

Trip 2. MARIN HEADLANDS
❶ Battery 129, Parking Area
❷ Point Bonita Lighthouse
❸ Rodeo Beach

1 Mile

Highway 101

Visitor Center

Tennessee Pt.

❸

Rodeo Lagoon

Bunker Road

McCullough Rd.

Alexander Ave.

Cavallo Pt.

Conzelman Rd.

❶

Bird Is.

Bonita Cove

Kirby Cove

Golden Gate Bridge

Pt. Diablo

Pt. Bonita

❷

The Marin Headlands are formed from pillow basalt, red chert, and sandstone of the Marin Headlands terrane of the Franciscan. This photo looks west across Bonita Cove to the Point Bonita Lighthouse. The rocks in Bonita Cove are mainly sandstone. The lighthouse is on a peninsula made up of pillow basalt.

Trip 2.
MARIN HEADLANDS
A Look at the Farallon Plate

The Marin Headlands are made up of some unusual Franciscan rocks called the *Marin Headlands terrane*. These rocks are mainly pillow basalt, red chert and sandstone and were once the ocean floor of the Farallon plate. When these rocks were formed, the Farallon plate was very large, and underlay most of the eastern Pacific Ocean. During the subduction process, almost all of the Farallon plate was devoured as it crept eastward into the Franciscan subduction zone. As these rocks were crammed into the subduction zone, they were broken into numerous thin fault slices, so they now lay scattered around the Marin Headlands like pieces of cucumbers, tomatoes, and cauliflower in a giant salad.

During the trip to the Marin Headlands you will see examples of all of the major rock types of the Marin Headlands terrane. At Battery 129 you will see some of the most spectacular exposures of red chert that can be seen anywhere in the world. The Point Bonita Lighthouse is built on pillow basalt, and you can see excellent pillows in the sea cliff immediately under the lighthouse. Finally, at the north end of Rodeo Beach you will see good exposures of the thick-bedded sandstones that occur in the Marin Headlands terrane.

The trip to the Marin Headlands can easily be done by car in one day, with time to enjoy many of the other attractions in the headlands. To reach the Marin Headlands from San Francisco, cross the Golden Gate Bridge and take the Alexander Ave. off-ramp just beyond the view plaza. Turn left at Alexander Ave, go beneath the freeway and follow the signs into the Marin Headlands. As you drive into the headlands you will be on Conzelman Road.

The Marin Headlands are in the Golden Gate National Recreation Area. For information on the Marin Headlands go to the visitor center at the head of Rodeo Lagoon (Phone 415-331-1540).

Farallon Plate

The pillow basalt, red chert, and sandstone that make up the Marin Headlands terrane once formed oceanic floor of the Farallon plate. The pillow basalt was formed when magma flowed out from the East Pacific Rise spreading center when the spreading center was far west of the North American continent. The chert was derived from silica-rich seawater and was deposited on top of the pillow basalt as the pillow basalt moved away from the spreading center. The pillow basalt and red chert were then carried eastward on the Farallon plate, as if on a conveyer belt, and the sandstone was deposited on top of the chert as the Farallon plate approached the North American continent. The sandstone was derived from erosion of rocks on the continent. As the pillow basalt, chert, and sandstone were carried into the Franciscan subduction zone, they were severely folded and faulted and cut into numerous thin fault slices.

During Tertiary time, the rocks of the Marin Headlands terrane were uplifted out of the subduction zone to form mountains and the rocks were subjected to erosion. The uplift and erosion of these rocks is still in progress. Each of the different types of rocks in the Marin Headlands terrane erodes in a different manner, so that there is a close relationship between the different types of rocks and the topography. The basalt, which is quite resistant to marine erosion, forms most of the points around the Marin Headlands, including Cavallo Point, Lime Point, Point Diablo, Point Bonita, Bird Island and Tennessee Point. The red chert is highly fractured and easily eroded by ocean waves, so that it forms coves along the shoreline. However, it forms hilltops and the crests inland, where it is resistant to erosion. The sandstone is resistant to erosion both along the shoreline and inland if the beds are thick, but is easily eroded where beds are thin and interbedded with silt and shale. The ridge that supports Battery Wallace is formed from thick resistant sandstones, whereas the valley occupied by Rodeo Lagoon is carved from soft thin sandstone and shale. The Marin Headlands are a patchwork of these different types of rocks.

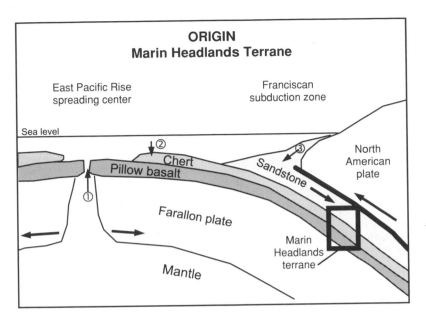

ORIGIN
Marin Headlands Terrane

The Marin Headlands terrane consists of three very different types of rocks — pillow basalt, chert, and sandstone:

① The pillow basalt was formed from magma rising from the East Pacific Rise spreading center.

② The chert was deposited on top of the pillow basalt from silica-saturated seawater while the spreading center was far from any land areas.

③ The sandstone was derived from the North American plate and deposited on top of the chert as the Farallon plate entered the Franciscan subduction zone.

ROCK TYPES
Marin Headlands Terrane

Locality	Rock Unit	Description
Battery 129	Red Chert	Thinly banded layers of hard red chert and soft red clay; the red chert fractures into sharp tabular plates a few inches across.
Point Bonita Lighthouse	Pillow Basalt	Dark green on fresh surfaces; red, brown, or yellow where weathered; well-defined pillows in some places.
Rodeo Beach	Sandstone	White or buff colored; composed of sand grains cemented to form hard rock.

Battery 129

Battery 129, also known as Construction 129, is on a hill that is formed of red chert of the Marin Headlands terrane. This hill is a classic viewpoint for Golden Gate Bridge. In September and October, thousands of migrating birds of prey concentrate at this hill, called Hawk Hill, before crossing the Golden Gate. Battery 129 is on Conzelman Road 1.8 miles west of the intersection of Conzelman Road and Alexander Road. The red chert is well-exposed in the parking area for the Battery.

● *Parking Area*

At the north end of parking area the chert rests on pillow basalt, just as it did when it was deposited on the sea floor during early Jurassic time 150 million years ago. This red chert is also referred to as ribbon chert for its characteristic alternating layers of hard red chert and soft red shale. The chert layers are about two inches thick, and the red shale layers are ususally less than one-half inch thick.

The chert is composed of silicon dioxide, the same chemical composition as window glass. It formed when hot ocean water in the vicinity of the spreading center became saturated with silica derived from the volcanic activity along the spreading center. As the seawater cooled it could no longer hold all of the silica, so the silica was deposited on the sea floor as a gel. The silica-saturated seawater also supported a large number of Radiolaria, one-celled floating animals that live in seawater and have a silica shell. As the Radiolaria died, their shells fell to the sea floor and were incorporated into the silica gel. With a magnifying glass you can see the Radiolaria as very small white specks in the chert. Radiolaria commonly make up from 10% to 50% of the chert. The formation of the red chert in this manner was slow, so that most beds of red chert are only a few tens of feet to a few hundred feet thick. Most of the chert was formed far from land areas because sediments from nearby land areas would have drowned out the chert.

The red shale between the chert layers is fine mineral dust from the atmosphere that fell into the ocean and accumulated in the silica gel on the sea floor. The thin layers of red shale segregated from the silica as the silica hardened into chert.

Small sharp folds can be seen in many outcrops of red chert. Some of these folds may have occurred by slumping of the still soft chert beds and others by later deformation of the hard chert in the subduction zone.

The layers of red chert in this road cut near Battery 129 were horizontal when deposited, but were later sharply folded, probably while the rocks were in the Franciscan subduction zone.

This photo shows thin bands of hard red chert about two inches thick alternating with thinner layers of soft red shale. The chert has been bent into a small fold along the axis of the hammer.

Point Bonita Lighthouse

It is usually difficult to see good pillows in pillow basalts because the rocks are commonly highly weathered and the outlines of the pillows are obscure. However, you can see some good pillows at the Point Bonita Lighthouse. To get to the lighthouse from Battery 129, continue west 2.3 miles on the one-way road to the parking area for the lighthouse, then follow the half-mile path to the lighthouse. The lighthouse is open seasonally on weekends. Call 415-331-1540 for hours and information. Try to get to the lighthouse when it is open; but if it is closed, you can still see some good pillows along the path to the lighthouse.

●Lighthouse

To see some excellent examples of pillow basalt, follow the path through the tunnel to the lighthouse. Before crossing the suspension bridge to the lighthouse, look at the rocks in the surf zone to the left of the lighthouse. You will see a large dark-green rock on the other side of a small sea arch. This rock is about 20 feet thick and 50 feet high, and is made up of a number of pillows a foot or so in diameter and a couple of feet long. You can see the rounded outlines of the pillows that have been etched by the constant wave action. These pillows were formed during Jurassic time when basaltic magma flowed out onto the sea floor from the East Pacific Rise spreading center when the spreading center was far west of the North American continent. As the basalt magma came into contact with the seawater, the outer margin of the magma chilled before crystals could form, giving the pillow a fine-grained outer rim. The fluid magma in the center of the pillow would break through the chilled rim and form another pillow, and so on. As the pillows were extruded onto the sea floor from the spreading center, the pillows were stacked one above the other so that the bottom of each pillow conformed to the convex top of the underlying pillow. Each new pillow added to the top of the stack was sufficiently mobile to mold itself to the irregular surface below.

On your return from the lighthouse, look at the rocks along the path immediately beyond the tunnel. Note the large rounded pillows in these rocks. As you continue on the path you will see many other basaltic rocks, including basalt flows without pillows, diabase dikes, tuffs, and agglomerates. The diabase dikes formed from basaltic magma that cooled in fractures before reaching the sea floor. The tuffs formed from ash thrown up into the air during volcanic eruptions. The agglomerates formed from loose volcanic rocks caught up in the basalt flows. It is difficult to distinguish these different types of volcanic rocks when the rocks are highly weathered.

The Point Bonita Lighthouse rests on a foundation of pillow basalt. The pillows are well-exposed on the rock in the surf zone on the other side of the sea arch.

This photo shows the rock at the sea arch in more detail. Constant wave action has conveniently etched the rock to show the rounded outlines of individual pillows. The thick layer of pillow basalt is tilted steeply to the right.

Rodeo Beach

Rodeo Beach is the easiest place to reach the beach in the Marin Headlands. Here you will have an opportunity to see good examples of the different rocks that make up the Marin Headlands terrane. At the north end of Rodeo Beach, you will see exposures of the sandstone that makes up most of the ridge that runs from Battery Wallace to Rodeo Lagoon. Along the main part of Rodeo Beach, you will see many pebbles of red chert along with the sand that forms the beach. If lucky, you may find some semi-precious carneleans among these pebbles. At the south end of the beach you will see thin fault slivers of the many different types of rocks that make up the Marin Headlands terrane.

To get to Rodeo Beach from the Point Bonita Lighthouse, continue on the loop road past Battery Alexander and the Marin Headlands visitor center. Turn left just beyond the visitor center, follow the signs to Rodeo Beach and park.

●North End

The cliffs at the north end of Rodeo Beach consist of sandstone. The beds are several feet thick and tilted steeply. Because the sandstone exposures are fresh, you can see grading and cross bedding in the sandstone. The sandstone also contains fragments of clay and volcanic rocks. Like the sandstones in the Alcatraz terrane and the San Bruno Mountain terrane, these sandstones were derived from erosion of the rocks of the North American plate and dumped on the top of the Farallon plate as it approached the North American plate.

●Rodeo Beach

The sand that forms Rodeo Beach is a good place to look for interesting pebbles that have eroded from the basalt and chert along the shoreline. Note the large amount of dark red pebbles on the beach. These have eroded from the red chert that is exposed on the hillsides and along the shoreline at the Marin Headlands. The pebbles have been rounded by the wave action, just as if placed in a rock tumbler. Among these pebbles, if you look hard and are lucky, are carnelians, a semi-precious translucent red-to-orange type of chalcedony, which is a form of quartz. The carnelians originally formed when silica-rich groundwater filled small round cavities in the basalt, called vesicles, that were caused by expanding gas while the basalt was still fluid. When the pillow basalt was subjected to weathering, the other components of the basalt broke down into sand and clay, leaving behind the hard carnelians.

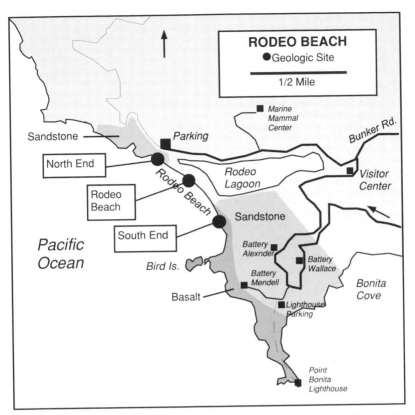

Rodeo Beach is at the mouth of Rodeo Lagoon. The lagoon was formed in an old river valley that was drowned as this part of the California coast subsided over the last million years. There are few lagoons like this along the California coast since most of the other parts of the northern California coast have been uplifted rather than drowned.

● *South End*

The cliffs at the south end of Rodeo Beach are formed from thinly faulted slivers of basalt, diabase, chert, and sandstone. Here you will see some fresh exposures of pillow basalt up close, which you could not do at the Point Bonita Lighthouse. The following rocks are encountered as you go southward along the cliff:

1. red chert,
2. sandstone and siltstone; repeated several times by faulting,
3. mixed pillow basalt and chert,
4. large sandstone blocks, probably from a landslide,
5. a promontory of pillow basalt that blocks further access to the south.

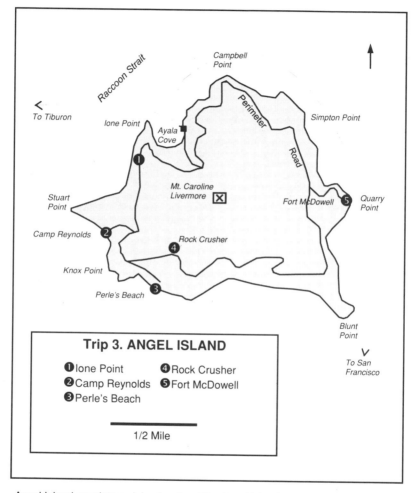

Raccoon Strait

Campbell
Point

To Tiburon

Ione Point

Perimeter

Simpton Point

Ayala
Cove

Road

Stuart
Point

Mt. Caroline
Livermore ⊠

Fort McDowell

Quarry
Point

Camp Reynolds

Rock Crusher

Knox Point

Perle's Beach

Blunt
Point

To San
Francisco

Trip 3. ANGEL ISLAND

❶ Ione Point ❹ Rock Crusher
❷ Camp Reynolds ❺ Fort McDowell
❸ Perle's Beach

1/2 Mile

Angel Island consists mainly of rocks of the Angel Island terrane of the Franciscan. These rocks differ from much of the Franciscan in that they are metamorphosed to the blueschist facies. Blueschists form only under the unusual conditions of extremely high pressures and relatively low temperatures that are characteristic of subduction zones.

Trip 3.
ANGEL ISLAND
Metamorphism and Blue Schists

Most Franciscan rocks have not been metamorphosed; that is, the pressures and temperatures in the subduction zone were not high enough to alter the rocks significantly. However, the Franciscan rocks that make up Angel Island are metamorphosed. They have been altered by extreme high pressure in the subduction zone. These rocks must have been carried to greater depths in the subduction zone than most Franciscan rocks.

The metamorphic rocks on Angel Island are called the *Angel Island terrane*. These rocks were originally sandstone, pillow basalt and serpentine, but were altered to schistose sandstone, schists, blueschists, metamorphosed pillow basalt, and metamorphosed serpentine. The blueschists are of special interest because they form only in subduction zones, and are thus considered as an indicator of subduction zones. After the rocks of the Angel Island terrane were metamorphosed, they were thrust over unmetamorphosed sandstones of the Alcatraz terrane. This must have occurred later when the subduction zone had become cooler.

You will see examples of all of the metamorphic rocks of the Angel Island terrane during the trip to Angel Island: schistose sandstone at <u>Ione Point</u>, blueschists at <u>Camp Reynolds</u>, schists and metamorphosed pillow basalt at <u>Perle's Beach</u>, and metamorphosed serpentine at the <u>Rock Crusher</u>. At <u>Camp Reynolds</u>, you will see the unmetamorphosed rocks of the Alcatraz terrane as well as the thrust fault that separates these rocks from the overlying rocks of the Angel Island terrane.

Allow one day for the trip. All of the geologic localities are on or near the Perimeter Road, which makes a five-mile circuit of the island. If possible, try to get to the island during low tide to see the rocks along the shoreline. Angel Island is a State Park with hiking trails, a museum, and a cafe at the ferry dock. The island is accessible by ferry from Fisherman's Wharf, Tiburon, or Vallejo. For information on logistics contact the Angel Island Company (415-897-0715).

Most of the rocks of the Angel Island terrane had only minor changes during metamorphism and the original rock types are still apparent. The schistose sandstone looks like a sandstone that has been squeezed, and the pillow basalt and serpentine appear almost unchanged. However, the schists and blueschists have been so highly metamorphosed that all traces of the original rocks were obliterated. Moreover, the blueschists contain unusual blue metamorphic minerals that form only under conditions of abnormally high pressure and relatively low temperature. Since these abnormal pressure and temperature conditions occur only in subduction zones, the blueschists are considered as indicators of subduction zones.

Rocks of the Angel Island terrane occur along the southern shoreline of the Tiburon Peninsula and in the Berkeley Hills as well as at Angel Island. Metamorphism of a widespread rock unit like the Angel Island terrane is rare in the Franciscan. Metamorphosed Franciscan rocks usually occur as individual boulders in melanges or as small isolated areas of moderate- to high-grade metamorphism.

ROCK TYPES
Angel Island Terrane

Locality	Rock Unit	Description
Ione Point (Perimeter Road)	Schistose sandstone	Sandstone with well developed schistosity; appears platy; sand grains still recognizable; some flattened pebbles.
Perle's Beach (West End)	Pillow basalt	Pillow basalt may be brown, yellow or dark green; well-defined pillows in some places; original feldspar and pyroxene altered to microscopic metamorphic minerals such as lawsonite and glaucophane.
Rock Crusher (Serpentine Quarry)	Serpentine	Green and very light green to white; slippery; foliated with ovoid masses of hard serpentine; occurs as craggy green outcrops.
Perle's Beach (East End)	Schist	Dark blue, brown, white; breaks into platy fragments; usually found as thin layers within pillow basalt or along the contacts between basalt or serpentine and other rocks.
Camp Reynolds (South End of Beach)	Blueschist	Schist with pronounced dark blue color; contains blue metamorphic minerals formed under conditions of very high pressure and relatively low temperature.

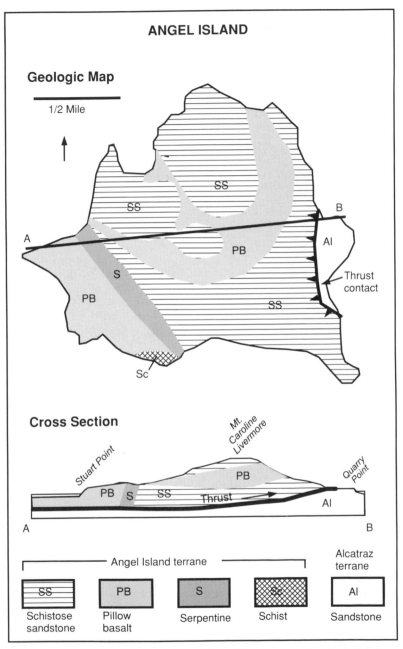

This geologic map shows the distribution of the different types of rocks that make up Angel Island. The cross section shows the surface along which the Angel Island terrane has been thrust over the Alcatraz terrane.

Ione Point

Most of the central and eastern parts of Angel Island consist of schistose sandstone of the Angel Island terrane. These rocks also form the crest of Mt. Caroline Livermore as well as Ione Point, Campbell Point, Simpton Point, and Blunt Point. The schistose sandstone is covered by vegetation over most of the interior of the island and is not well exposed. However, there are good exposures of the schistose sandstone in the road cuts along the Perimeter Road just south of Ione Point.

●Perimeter Road

To get to the Perimeter Road from the ferry dock, follow the path that goes west near the shoreline. This path connects with the Perimeter Road just south of Ione Point. The road cuts along the Perimeter Road for the next 800 feet to the south are in schistose sandstone.

This schistose sandstone was formed from graywacke sandstone that was subjected to a moderate grade of metamorphism. The grains of the original sandstone are still apparent, but the sand grains have been flattened by the high pressure that they were subjected to in the Franciscan subduction zone. If you look at a piece of the schistose sandstone with a magnifying glass you will see that it is composed of very thin layers of small flattened grains. These layers are parallel to the original bedding of the graywacke sandstone. The tendency of the rock to break into tabular pieces is called *schistosity*. The schistosity dips steeply to the north and west, indicating that the rocks were tilted in that direction some time after deposition.

In some places, pebbles can still be seen in the sandstone, and the pebbles are also flattened parallel to the schistosity. Look for some of these pebbles in the road cuts about 750 feet south of where you started walking on the Perimeter Road.

Although it is not apparent by looking at the sandstone, new metamorphic minerals have replaced many of the original grains in the sandstone. These minerals can be seen with the aid of a microscope when looking at a very thin slice of the sandstone. The metamorphic minerals include lawsonite, jadeitic pyroxene, aragonite, and crossite. These minerals were formed by altering the composition of the original grains that made up the sandstone. Studies have shown that the new minerals were formed by rearranging the material already in the rock, and without the addition of materials from outside the sandstone.

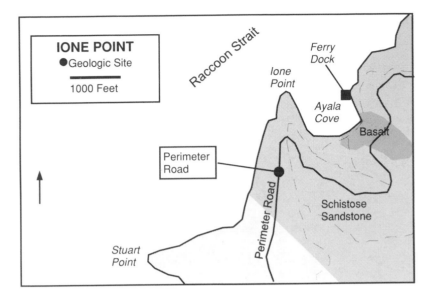

Ione Point, on the west side of Ayala Cove, is made up of schistose sandstone of the Angel Island terrane. The thin layering of the schistose sandstone can be seen in the road cuts along the Perimeter Road near Ione Point. This is the most common rock on Angel Island, but there are few good exposures.

Camp Reynolds

There are two geologic sites at Camp Reynolds, the seawall which has good examples of honeycomb weathering, and the south end of the beach where you will see some blueschists that are formed only in subduction zones.

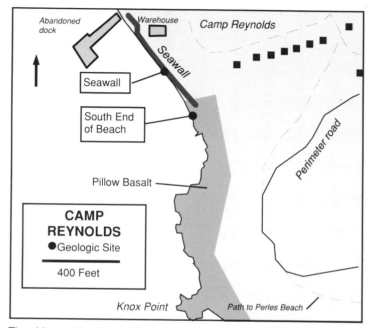

The old seawall at Camp Reynolds has excellent examples of honeycomb weathering. At the south end of the beach are good exposures of pillow basalt with seams of blueschist.

● Seawall

To get to Camp Reynolds from Ione Point, continue southwest on the Perimeter Road 0.5 miles to Camp Reynolds, then follow the path to the old warehouse near the abandoned dock. The seawall extends along the shoreline to the south of the warehouse. The seawall was constructed between 1864 and 1877, mainly from sandstone from Quarry Point at Fort McDowell. The sandstone blocks in the lower part of the seawall have not been eroded to any significant degree, even though these blocks are subject to wave attack at high tide. The sandstone blocks at the top of the seawall are above high tide, but are constantly subjected to sea spray. The blocks subjected to the sea spray have been etched into an intricate honeycomb pattern of pits and holes. The etching is thought to have been caused by salt crystal growth during evaporation of the sea spray. The

Honeycomb weathering occurs in the sandstone blocks in the splash zone of the seawall at Camp Reynolds. This unusual weathering is caused by salt crystals prying sand grains out of the sandstone as the sea water evaporates. The sun glasses provide scale.

new and constantly forming salt crystals wedge out the sand grains from the sandstone thereby forming pits on the surface of the sandstone. The seawall also contains boulders of gabbro and granite along with the sandstone. These boulders have not been affected by the sea spray. The sandstone that has been etched by the sea spray has retreated as much as six inches from the surface as defined by the gabbro and granite boulders, indicating an etching rate of about one-half inch per decade. Similar honeycomb weathering can be found all along the California north coast where thick sandstones are subjected to sea spray. Salt Point State Park in Sonoma County has some excellent examples of this type of weathering.

● South End of Beach

Follow the seawall to the south end of the beach. The rocks exposed along the bluff just south of the seawall are mainly pillow basalt. Within the pillow basalt there are some thin seams of deep blueschist an inch or so thick. In its former life, this blueschist was chert that had been interbedded with the basalt. The chert was altered to blueschist in the subduction zone. Look for flat pebbles of the blueschist in the pebbles along the shore at the south end of the seawall. These pebbles have been eroded from the seams of blueschist interlayered with the pillow basalt.

Perle's Beach

Perle's Beach lies near the contact between a thick unit of serpentine that cuts northwest across Angel Island and the pillow basalts that form the west end of Angel Island. A number of different types of schists have been formed along this contact zone, and these schists are well exposed in the sea cliffs at the east end of Perle's Beach. The pillow basalts that form the western part of Angel Island can be seen in the sea cliffs at the west end of the beach. To get to Perle's Beach from Camp Reynolds, continue south on the Perimeter Road 0.25 miles and take the path to the beach. The beach is about 200 yards long.

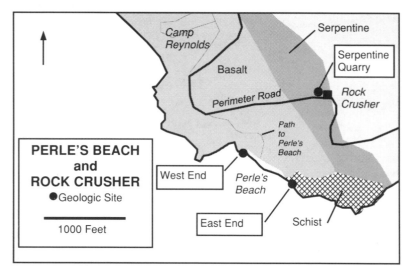

At the east end of Perle's Beach there are several different types of schist. These are the most highly metamorphosed rocks on Angel Island. The schists formed along the contact zone between pillow basalt and serpentine. The easy exchange of matter along this contact zone accelerated metamorphism.

● East End

The rocks at the east end of the beach are mainly layers of schists that have been highly metamorphosed. These rocks lie near the contact between the pillow basalts that form the west part of Angel Island and the thick belt of serpentine exposed at the serpentine quarry. The first rocks that jut out into the beach are serpentine. The serpentine is foliated and the foliations wrap around ovoid masses of harder serpentine. Further east, the serpentine contains large blocks of sandstone. Still further east, the serpentine is in contact with brown schist that is thinly layered with a dark blue quartz-rich rock. The brown schist was likely shale before it was metamorphosed, and the dark blue quartz-rich rock was probably chert that had been interbedded with the shale. There are also some layers of blueschist at the east end of the beach. The blueschists get their deep blue color from the abundant blue minerals that were formed during metamorphism. The blue minerals, which include lawsonite and glaucophane, are formed only at abnormally high pressure and relatively low temperature, conditions found only in subduction zones. These conditions occur when cool rocks have been rapidly plunged to great depths and subjected to high pressure in the subduction zone and then uplifted before the rocks can be heated to the high temperatures usually found at those great depths. Laboratory studies show that these blue minerals form at pressures equivalent to rock burial depths of 12 to 30 miles and at temperatures of 100 to 300 degrees C. Normal temperatures at these depths are well over 300 degrees C.

The rocks that have been metamorphosed under these unusual conditions are referred to by geologists as the *blueschist facies*. Although all of the rocks in the Angel Island terrane are in the blueschist facies, they are not all colored blue, since most of the rocks contain only small amounts of the blue metamorphic minerals.

● West End

The southwest part of Angel Island is formed from pillow basalt. These rocks are well exposed at the west end of Perle's Beach. The pillow basalt occurs in layers a few feet thick and these layers dip steeply to the northwest. The best pillows are in the rocks at the extreme west end of the beach and can be reached only at low tide. Look for pillow-shaped masses a foot or so in diameter in these brown-colored rocks. In places, the pillow basalts are separated by layers of chert or other metamorphic rocks.

Although not apparent in a hand specimen, the pillow basalt is also metamorphosed to the blueschist facies. Microscopic studies show that the original basalt consisted mainly of pyroxene and plagioclase feldspar. Much of the original pyroxene and feldspar have been replaced by very small crystals of metamorphic minerals. The feldspar has altered to chlorite, lawsonite, crossite and jadeite. The pyroxene has been partly replaced by chlorite, glaucophane and green jadeite.

This photo shows a bed of pillow basalt exposed in the bluff at the west end of Perle's Beach. The pencil provides scale and rests on top of one of the elongated pillows.

The rock crusher at the serpentine quarry near Perle's Beach was used to crush the serpentine. The crushed serpentine was used for road building on Angel Island.

Rock Crusher

On the western part of Angel Island there is a northwest-trending belt of serpentine that is several hundred feet thick. This belt of serpentine separates the pillow basalts that form the westernmost part of the island from the schistose sandstones that form the central and eastern parts of the island. One of the best places to see this serpentine is at the serpentine quarry next to the rock crusher near Perle's Beach. The serpentine is also exposed along the shoreline east of Perle's Beach, but access to this part of the beach is difficult and not recommended.

●Serpentine Quarry

To get to the serpentine quarry from Perle's Beach, continue east 0.25 miles on the Perimeter Road to the quarry. The quarry is flanked by a large rock crusher that is no longer in operation. The crushed serpentine was used for road building on Angel Island and for construction of a dam to the east of the quarry. If you look through the holes in the asphalt pavement along the Perimeter Road, you can see the green serpentine rocks that were used as the road base in many places.

The serpentine in the quarry is pale green, feels very slippery, and is intensely foliated. This foliated serpentine contains ovoid masses of very dense serpentine, usually darker green in color. In places there are also ovoid masses of other rocks within the serpentine, including gabbro, sandstone, and metamorphic rocks. Some of these metamorphic rocks were formed by alteration of basalt or diabase inclusions within the serpentine.

The belt of serpentine exposed at the serpentine quarry is the largest unit of serpentine on Angel Island. This serpentine represents a chunk of oceanic crust that was incorporated into the Angel Island terrane, probably as the Angel Island terrane was being digested in the Franciscan subduction zone. Other small blocks of serpentine occur in several places on Angel Island, mainly within the pillow basalts from Perle's Beach to Camp Reynolds.

For more details on the origin of serpentine refer to the Fort Point geologic site on the trip to San Francisco. You will also see more serpentine during the geologic trip to Ring Mountain.

Fort McDowell

After the Angel Island terrane was emplaced in the Franciscan subduction zone, the Alcatraz terrane was carried into the subduction zone and thrust under the Angel Island terrane. The rocks along the zone of thrusting were ground up to form a layer of clay and rounded boulders. Fort McDowell is sprawled across this zone of thrusting. Quarry Point is formed from rocks of the Alcatraz terrane below the thrust. The Enlisted Men's Barracks and Parade Grounds lie within the zone of thrusting. The Officers Row above the Parade Grounds is situated on the Angel Island terrane above the thrust. At Fort McDowell you will go to the Guard House near Quarry Point where you can stand in the zone of thrusting and see good exposures of the Alcatraz sandstone in the sandstone quarry below the thrust.

● Guard House

To get to the Guard House at Fort McDowell from the serpentine quarry, continue east on the Perimeter Road 2.0 miles to Fort McDowell then follow the path to the dock at Quarry Point. The Guard House is near the dock. There is a visitor center in the Guard House. Go to the backyard of the Guard House, where you can get a good view of the quarry. The

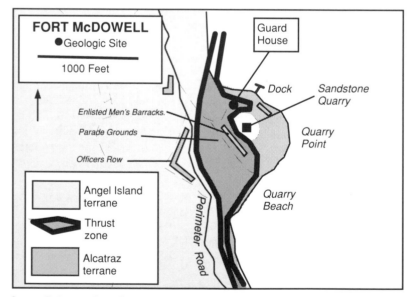

Quarry Point consists of sandstones of the Alcatraz terrane. These rocks underlie and are separated from the Angel Island terrane by a thrust fault that extends from Quarry Beach to north of Quarry Point.

This photo shows the Alcatraz sandstone in the quarry at Quarry Point. The Enlisted Men's Barracks is at the right side of the photo. The flat surface that the Enlisted Men's Barracks is built on is the thrust fault between the Alcatraz terrane and the Angel Island terrane.

quarry is fenced off, but you can see that the rocks in the quarry are thick-bedded and similar to the Alcatraz sandstone on Alcatraz Island.

The zone of thrusting that separates the Alcatraz sandstone from the Angel Island terrane is nearly flat and consists of a melange several tens of feet thick. The melange is difficult to see because the clay is soft and easily eroded. What you can see is the nearly flat surface formed by the hard rocks of the Alcatraz terrane that forms the lower boundary of the thrust zone. At the top of the quarry you are standing on this surface. The Enlisted Men's Barracks and the Parade Grounds west of the barracks also lie on this surface. From the barracks, the thrust zone slopes gently to the north and intersects the beach just north of Quarry Point. To the south, the zone of thrusting lies just above Quarry Beach and intersects the shoreline further south toward Blunt Point.

It is somewhat unusual for metamorphosed rocks to overlie unmetamorphosed rocks. It appears that the rocks of the Angel Island terrane reached the Franciscan subduction zone first and became metamorphosed during the earlier and hotter stages of subduction. The rocks of the Alcatraz terrane were inserted under the Angel Island terrane later when the subduction zone was cooler.

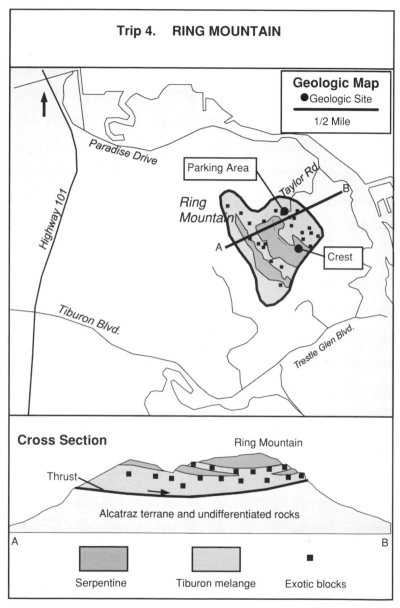

Trip 4. RING MOUNTAIN

Geologic Map
●Geologic Site
1/2 Mile

Paradise Drive

Parking Area

Taylor Rd

Ring Mountain

B

Highway 101

A

Crest

Tiburon Blvd.

Trestle Glen Blvd.

Cross Section

Ring Mountain

Thrust

Alcatraz terrane and undifferentiated rocks

A   B

Serpentine   Tiburon melange   Exotic blocks

The crest of Ring Mountain is formed from thick layers of serpentine. The Tiburon melange, immediately below the serpentine, contains large exotic blocks of unusual metamorphic rocks. The Tiburon melange was thrust over the Alcatraz terrane, which is exposed at the base of Ring Mountain.

Trip 4.
RING MOUNTAIN
Exotic Blocks - Thermometers in the Subduction Zone

Ring Mountain is geologically similar to Angel Island in that Franciscan metamorphic rocks have been thrust over unmetamorphosed rocks of the Alcatraz terrane. The Alcatraz terrane can be found on the lower slopes of Ring Mountain, whereas metamorphosed rocks and serpentine occur on the upper slopes and crest. The metamorphosed rocks at Ring Mountain occur as large boulders, or *exotic blocks*, in the Tiburon melange. These exotic blocks are of special interest to geologists because they have acted like digital thermometers that have been inserted into the bowels of the Franciscan subduction zone, and thus provide a record of temperatures and pressures in the subduction zone.

The trip to Ring Mountain can be easily done from San Francisco in half a day. During the trip you will go to the parking area at the end of Taylor Road, where you will examine some exotic blocks. You will then follow a short trail to the crest of the mountain where you will see the thick slab of serpentine that forms the flat top of the mountain.

Ring Mountain lies within the Ring Mountain Preserve and is administered by The Nature Conservancy (Phone 415-435-6465). There are many unusual plants on the preserve that grow there because of the serpentine soils. You can see many of these plants on the 1.5-mile self-guided loop trail into the preserve that leaves from the parking area on Paradise Drive, 0.8 miles west of Taylor Road.

Taylor Road
To get to Taylor Road, go north on Highway 101 from the Golden Gate Bridge to the Paradise Drive exit 7.0 miles north of the Golden Gate Bridge. Turn right on Paradise Drive and keep sharply to the right to stay on Paradise Drive. Continue east 2.3 miles to Taylor Road, turn right on Taylor Road and go 0.5 miles to the end of Taylor Road. Turn right into the public parking area at the end of the road and park. This parking area is the first geologic site and the paved fire road from the parking area goes to the geologic site at the crest of the mountain.

●*Parking Area*

In and adjacent to the parking area at the end of Taylor Road there are a number of large isolated boulders of varying size. Some of these boulders are a foot or so across, and some the size of a small house. These boulders are exotic blocks in the Tiburon melange. The soft clay of the Tiburon melange has been washed away and left the exotic blocks on the surface of the ground likes plums in a plum pudding. The clay that forms the matrix of the melange consists of rocks that were ground into a fine powder by the thrusting action within the subduction zone. You will not see any good exposures of this clay since it is too soft to form outcrops.

Take a good look at the exotic blocks in and near the parking area. You will find that some of the blocks have grooves that were formed as the blocks rubbed against other rocks during their wanderings in the subduction zone. Other blocks have a rind of chlorite, talc, or other minerals. These minerals are slippery and served as a lubricant as the blocks were squeezed through the melange. Most of the blocks sparkle from flakes of mica that were formed during metamorphism. Almost all of the blocks appear to have rough, platy layers. This layering, called schistosity, formed during metamorphism as the different minerals segregated into layers.

The large exotic block in the center of this photo is adjacent to the parking lot at the end of Taylor Road. The fire road to the right leads to the serpentine exposures at the crest of the mountain.

The exotic blocks at Ring Mountain offer one of the best places in the Coast Ranges for the study of Franciscan metamorphism because of the wide variety of metamorphic rocks found in the blocks. Some of the more common metamorphic rocks include amphibolites, eclogites, and blueschists. The amphibolites have dark elongated crystals, sometimes up to two inches long. The blueschists appear as very dark blue layers within the schists. The eclogites have small red crystals of garnet.

Many of the metamorphic minerals in these rocks, like lawsonite, glaucophane and garnet, form only under very specific conditions of pressure and temperature. Some of the minerals also provide a record of when the metamorphism occurred, based on the rate of decay of radioactive isotopes in the minerals. Using the age, temperature and pressure information from these minerals, it is possible for specialized geologists to reconstruct the pressure-temperature history of the Franciscan subduction zone.

On the basis of the age, temperature and pressure information from the blocks, subduction of the Franciscan is thought to have begun in early Jurassic time, about 175 million years ago. At the beginning of subduction, sedimentary and igneous rocks on the Farallon plate were metamorphosed at high temperatures as they were brought into the subduction zone and carried below the North American plate. Some of the weaker rocks in the subduction zone were crushed to form the clay melange while some of the very hard metamorphic rocks were broken into pieces and remained as large, hard blocks within the melange. With continuing subduction, the rocks in the subduction zone cooled because of the influx of the cool, wet rocks from the sea floor of the Farallon plate. Some of the blocks in the melange continued to be carried to greater depths in the cooler subduction zone. Glaucophane and lawsonite were formed under these low temperature-high pressure conditions by chemical alteration of the original amphiboles and feldspars. About 65 million years ago subduction ended, and the Coast Ranges were uplifted and eroded. Eventually this uplift and erosion brought the exotic blocks to the surface, where they now lie scattered on the landscape as if placed in a large rock garden.

Exotic blocks with high-grade metamorphic minerals like the blocks at Ring Mountain are widespread in the Franciscan of the Coast Ranges, but make up less that one percent of the Franciscan. These blocks have also been referred to as knockers, tectonic blocks, or high-grade blocks.

The grooves in this exotic block near the parking area were formed as the block was squeezed through the Tiburon melange while the block was in the Franciscan subduction zone.

Most of the exotic blocks are schistose; that is, they appear platy on broken surfaces. Most of these fresh broken surfaces are covered by sparkling flakes of mica. A lizard conveniently provides scale.

● *Crest*

Continue on the path to the crest of Ring Mountain. The round-trip hike is about half a mile. You will be on the Tiburon melange during most of the hike and see more exotic blocks along the road. As you approach the flat top of the mountain you will see that the crest is formed from two thick sub-horizontal layers of light yellow-brown serpentine. These layers represent coherent pieces of the ocean crust of the Farallon plate that were incorporated into the Tiburon melange. For more detail on how the serpentine was formed refer to the Fort Point locality on the geologic trip to San Francisco. Also refer to the discussion of spreading centers under Plate Tectonics.

The serpentine on the crest of Ring Mountain resists weathering and forms hard blocky outcrops. On fresh exposures, the rock is pale green, sometimes with dark specks about the size of small peas. These dark specks are remnants of pyroxene crystals that have been altered to serpentine.

In places, some large blocks of this serpentine have broken off and are slowly sliding down the side of the mountain, lubricated by the soft and slippery clay of the underlying Tiburon melange. Rainwater accumulates in fractures in the serpentine and makes its way down to the contact between the serpentine and the clay. Putting water along this contact zone is like putting wax on the runners of a ski.

Soils formed from serpentine are characterized by anomalous plant life. This is due to the composition of serpentine. Serpentine is mainly an iron and magnesium silicate. There is almost no aluminum, so no clay soil is formed and the soil is thin and gravelly. The serpentine also has toxic amounts of magnesium, nickel, chromium and cobalt, and is low in plant nutrients such as potassium, sodium, calcium, and phosphorus.

Most common plants avoid serpentine. However, a few hardy and specialized plants thrive under these conditions. Some of the unusual plants at Ring Mountain include Tiburon Indian paintbrush, Oakland Star tulip, and the very rare Tiburon Mariposa lily, whose only natural occurrence is at Ring Mountain. The Tiburon Mariposa lily is abundant at Ring Mountain and is found especially among the blocky serpentine boulders and outcrops where there are springs and where the lily is protected from grazing. The plant is about two feet high and blooms in May and June with cinnamon-and-yellow flowers.

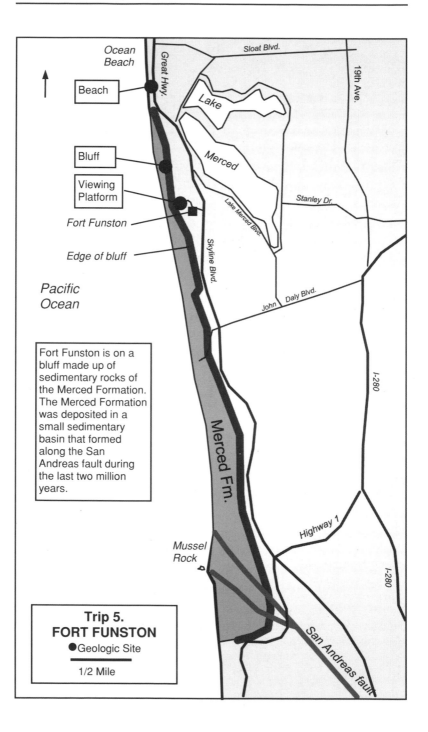

Ocean
Beach

Great Hwy.

Sloat Blvd.

19th Ave.

Beach

Lake

Merced

Bluff

Viewing
Platform

Fort Funston

Lake Merced Blvd.

Stanley Dr.

Edge of bluff

Skyline Blvd.

Pacific
Ocean

John   Daly Blvd.

Fort Funston is on a
bluff made up of
sedimentary rocks of
the Merced Formation.
The Merced Formation
was deposited in a
small sedimentary
basin that formed
along the San
Andreas fault during
the last two million
years.

I-280

Merced Fm.

Highway 1

Mussel
Rock

I-280

Trip 5.
FORT FUNSTON
●Geologic Site

1/2 Mile

San Andreas fault

Trip 5.
FORT FUNSTON
Recent and Ancient Beaches and Dunes

The Franciscan rocks are covered by a blanket of younger sedimentary rocks at many places in and around San Francisco. During the trip to Fort Funston you will learn how these sedimentary rocks were formed. The first stop is at <u>Ocean Beach,</u> where you will see how beach sand and sand dunes are presently being deposited along the shoreline. You will then continue to <u>Fort Funston,</u> where you will see how similar sedimentary rocks, called the Merced formation, were deposited in a small basin along the San Andreas fault about half-a-million years ago. The trip to Ocean Beach and Fort Funston should take about half a day.

Sedimentary rocks of the Merced Formation are exposed in the bluff at Fort Funston. These rock layers were deposited about half a million years ago along a shoreline very similar to the present shoreline along Ocean Beach.

Ocean Beach

Ocean Beach lies to your right as you drive along the Great Highway the four miles from Cliff House to Fort Funston. On your left, as you pass Golden Gate Park, you will see two large windmills. These windmills were originally used to pump water to a reservoir in Golden Gate Park for use in the park. The Murphy Windmill was built in 1905, and the Dutch Windmill was build somewhat later. The Dutch Windmill was restored in 1981, and is worth a visit. At the turn of the century, these windmills were at the leading edge of a large area of sand dunes that reached east from Ocean Beach through Golden Gate Park and covered much of northern San Francisco. It is hard to see these dunes now, since they are covered by buildings, roads and landscaping, but you may catch a glimpse of the dunes here and there in places like Golden Gate Park and the San Francisco Zoo.

The windmills were powered by the same prevailing westerly winds that carried the sand from Ocean Beach to downtown San Francisco. It is obvious that a huge quantity of sand was required to form Ocean Beach and these sand dunes. Yet there are no rivers currently supplying sand to Ocean Beach. So where did all of this sand come from and how did it get here?

The sand at Ocean Beach and in the sand dunes of northern San Francisco is really a relic, a gift from the past. These sands were deposited along the western shoreline of the San Francisco peninsula during the Wisconsin glacial period, from 10,000 to 15,000 years ago, when sea level was low and the Sacramento River flowed through the Golden Gate. If you had visited Ocean Beach at that time, you would not have seen this shoreline. Sea level was about 200 feet lower than now, there was no water in San Francisco Bay, and the shoreline was about 20 miles west of Ocean Beach. Large quantities of sand were carried from the Sierras by the Sacramento River and deposited to form beaches and dunes along this shoreline. As the glaciers melted, sea level rose and the shoreline, beach sand, and sand dunes moved eastward with the rise of sea level. Ocean Beach represents the present location of this shoreline. With falling sea level, the shoreline will retreat to the west, and with rising sea level, the shoreline will continue to move eastward.

In places, some of the old beach sands and sand dunes were overtaken and covered by the advancing sea. These areas now can be found as patches of sand several miles offshore. Potato Patch Shoal off the Golden Gate is an area of old sand dunes now covered by the ocean.

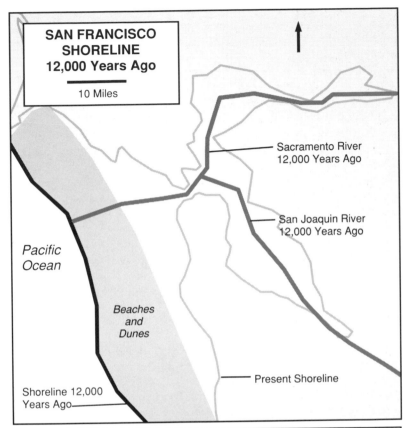

SAN FRANCISCO SHORELINE 12,000 Years Ago

10 Miles

Sacramento River 12,000 Years Ago

San Joaquin River 12,000 Years Ago

Pacific Ocean

Beaches and Dunes

Present Shoreline

Shoreline 12,000 Years Ago

GLACIAL CHRONOLOGY

Epoch	Glaciation	Interglacial	Years before present	Sea Level
Holocene			0 - 10,000	High
Pleistocene	Wisconsin		10,000 - 15,000	Low
		Sangamon	15,000 - 130,000	High
	Illinoisian		130,000 - 270,000	Low
		Yarmouth	270,000 - 350,000	High
	Kansan		350,000 - 600,000	Low
		Afton	600,000 - 1,000,000	High
	Nebraskan		1,000,000 - 2,000,000	Low

San Francisco Bay has been filled and emptied of sea water many times during the Pleistocene as sea level rose and fell in response to glacial advances and retreats.

● *Beach*

Stop anywhere along Ocean Beach and walk down to the beach. If you take a handful of sand and look at it with a magnifying glass, you'll see many different types of grains. These grains were formed from the different types of rocks that have been subjected to weathering and erosion in the drainage of the Sacramento River. Most of the clear grains and white grains are quartz and feldspar. Quartz and feldspar are two of the main constituents of granite, and these grains were derived from the weathering of granite in the Sierras. Quartz is extremely hard and feldspar is fairly hard. The quartz and feldspar grains easily survived the long and arduous trip from the Sierras down the Sacramento River, through the Golden Gate and into the Pacific. Most of the sand grains are rounded. The original grains were angular, but became rounded by constantly rubbing against each other as they were transported down the river and moved along the shoreline in the surf zone.

Note that most of the sand grains along the present beach are about the same size. If you look at the sand in several places, starting low in the surf zone then going higher up the beach, you will find that the grains in the lower part of the surf zone are smaller that those in the upper part. The grains have been neatly sorted by the wave action in the surf zone.

The wave action in the surf zone concentrates most of the sand in a narrow zone along the shoreline. Further offshore, in deeper water, the sea floor may be muddy, may have rock outcrops, or there may be patches of sand left over from earlier beaches or dunes that are now submerged. The sand along the shoreline is kept there by the wave action and by currents that carry the sand along the shoreline. High waves in winter will remove some of the sand from the beach and deposit it further offshore. Low summer waves will return the sand to the beaches, thus restoring the beaches. Storms will tear into one part of a beach and build up another part, and then redistribute the sand in another way in another storm. Sandy beaches are mother nature's sand box, and a tremendous amount of wave energy is invested in moving this sand from one place to another, and back again.

On the bluff at Fort Funston you will see some layers of sandstone that represent beaches and dunes that were formed several hundred thousand years ago. These ancient beach and dune sandstones were formed by depositional processes similar to those now in action at Ocean Beach.

This photo shows sand dunes at the south end of Ocean Beach near the San Francisco Zoo. At the turn of the century similar sand dunes covered much of northern San Francisco.

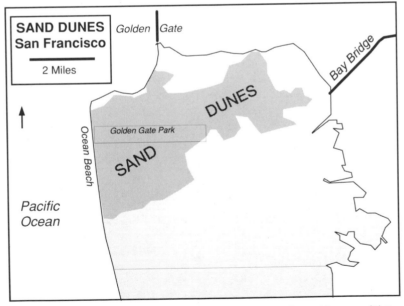

The sand dunes that covered much of San Francisco were formed from sand that was blown inland from Ocean Beach by the prevailing westerly winds. This sand was brought to Ocean Beach by the Sacramento River when it flowed through the Golden Gate during times of Pleistocene glaciation.

Fort Funston

To get to Fort Funston from Ocean Beach, continue south on the Great Highway to where it intersects Skyline Blvd. The entrance to Fort Funston is on Skyline Blvd. 0.7 miles south of this intersection. Fort Funston provided defense to San Francisco during World War I and World War II and in the cold war thereafter. Fort Funston is now part of the Golden National Recreation Area. The fort has excellent coastal views, short hiking trails, and is a favorite site for hang gliders. There is also a visitor center. For information, phone 417-556-8371.

● Viewing Platform

Park near the Viewing Platform at Fort Funston, and walk on out to the platform. The Viewing Platform lies at the edge of a steep bluff that faces the Pacific. Ocean breezes collide with the bluff, and in their effort to get over the bluff provide support for hang gliders and birds that effortlessly glide along the upwelling currents. Although the bluff may appear to have been here forever, in geologic terms it has been here only an instant. From the Viewing Platform we will consider how the bluff was formed.

The flat surface upon which the Viewing Platform, parking area, and the remainder of Fort Funston are situated is called a *marine terrace*. This terrace, which is now 150 feet above sea level, was cut by wave action during the Sangamon interglacial period, about 100,000 years ago, when sea level was higher than it is now.

As the climate became cooler during the Wisconsin glacial period, glaciers formed, sea level fell, and the shoreline retreated to the west of Fort Funston. The land along the shoreline was also uplifted slowly, a few tens of feet. By the end of the Wisconsin, about 10,000 years ago, the shoreline had retreated westward ten miles or more. As you stand on the Viewing Platform, imagine that there is no bluff and that the terrace you are standing on extended so far to the west that you cannot even see the Pacific Ocean.

As the Wisconsin glaciers began to melt during the last 10,000 years, sea level rose and the ocean began cutting a new wave-cut platform into the rocks along the shoreline at a lower level. The old wave-cut platform was separated from the new platform by a sea cliff, or bluff. As the new wave-cut platform cut further east, the bluff retreated east an inch or so a year until it arrived at its present position. The bluff is still being cut eastward, and in a few tens of years will claim the Viewing Platform and then Highway 1 sometime thereafter. The remaining part of the old wave-cut platform is now preserved as a marine terrace.

Marine terraces are common along the California coast north and south of San Francisco. The terraces were preserved because most of the California coastline has been slowly uplifted several hundred feet over the last million years. In general, the highest terraces are the oldest and were cut during the early interglacial stages, and the lowest terraces were cut during the late interglacial stages. Because there have been many fluctuations of sea level during the glacial period, and because the amount of uplift has varied along the coast, it is difficult to correlate specific terraces over long distances. There are no terraces between Fort Funston through the Marin Headlands. This area subsided during the Pleistocene. Indeed, there would be no San Francisco Bay if this area had been uplifted as were the areas to the north and south.

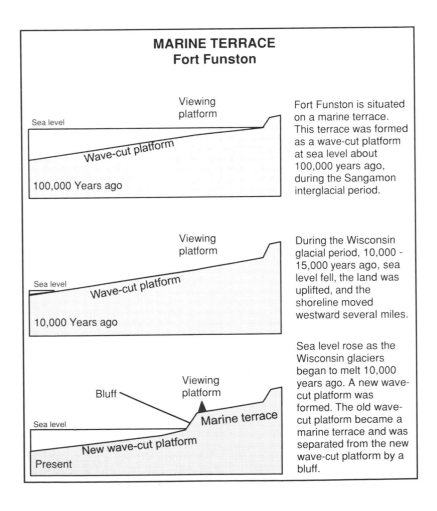

MARINE TERRACE
Fort Funston

Fort Funston is situated on a marine terrace. This terrace was formed as a wave-cut platform at sea level about 100,000 years ago, during the Sangamon interglacial period.

During the Wisconsin glacial period, 10,000 - 15,000 years ago, sea level fell, the land was uplifted, and the shoreline moved westward several miles.

Sea level rose as the Wisconsin glaciers began to melt 10,000 years ago. A new wave-cut platform was formed. The old wave-cut platform became a marine terrace and was separated from the new wave-cut platform by a bluff.

●*Bluff*

The bluff at Fort Funston is made up of sedimentary rocks that were deposited in a small sedimentary basin that had formed along the San Andreas fault during Pleistocene time. These sediments, called the Merced Formation, are exposed as distinct layers that can be seen along the bluff from Lake Merced southward to the San Andreas fault near Mussel Rock, a distance of about four miles. Some of the layers of sedimentary rocks are nearly horizontal and some are tilted to the north, indicating that the rocks have been uplifted and folded in the few hundred thousand years since they were deposited.

To get a good look at the rocks in the Merced Formation, follow the path south of the Viewing Platform down the bluff to the beach. Continue north along the beach to the Daly City sewer outlet 500 feet north of the Viewing Platform. Note that the rocks that form the bluff occur in layers from several inches to several feet thick. These layers are all sedimentary rocks, and include gravel, sandstone, siltstone and mudstone. The gravel has large pea-sized grains. The sandstone is mostly white and light gray and is made up of smaller sand-sized grains that are easily visible. The grains in the siltstone are too small to see without a magnifying glass, but the siltstone feels gritty. The claystone feels smooth and is medium-to-dark gray in color.

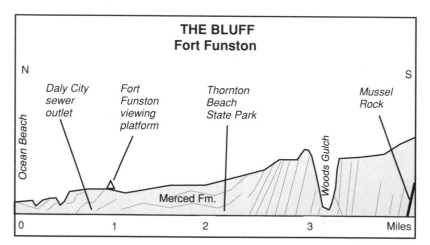

This cross section shows the rock layers in the Merced Formation that are exposed along the bluff from Fort Funston to Mussel Rock. The beds have been gently folded and generally dip to the north. The vertical scale is highly exaggerated.

The Daly City sewer outlet is at the left of this photo. Here, the Merced Formation consists of nearly-horizontal layers of gravel, sandstone, siltstone and mudstone. The gravel and sandstone were deposited mainly along ancient rivers and beaches, whereas the siltstone and mudstone were deposited in ancient bays or in deeper water offshore.

Each layer of rock in the bluff represents sediments that were deposited during a specific interval of geologic time. Most of the siltstone and fine-grained sandstone was deposited offshore as *marine sediments* in water depths of 30 to 300 feet. As these fine-grained sediments were being deposited offshore, coarser sand and gravel were being deposited along the shoreline. Further inland, *nonmarine sediments* were being deposited as sand dunes, as sand or mud along rivers, and as mud in swamps and coastal embayments.

Since the layers in the bluff alternate between marine, shoreline and nonmarine sediments, this shows that the shoreline of the Merced sea was constantly moving landward and seaward during deposition of the sediments. The movement of the shoreline depended on how fast the basin was subsiding, on the rate at which sediments were supplied to the basin, and on changes in sea level caused by the glacial and interglacial episodes of the Pleistocene. Landward movement of the shoreline is referred to as *transgression* and seaward movement as *regression*. During a transgression, layers of marine sediments extend inland. During a regression, layers of nonmarine sediments extend seaward. Dozens of transgressions and regressions of the sea are recorded in the sedimentary layers along the bluff.

The layer of silt and clay above the Daly City sewer outlet was deposited in a restricted bay landward of the shoreline. Look for shells of fossil mollusks in the clay. Directly above the silt and clay is a thin layer of coarse sand and pebbles. This sandstone marks an eastward transgression of the shoreline over the earlier bay sediments. The fine-grained sand above the coarse sand was deposited in shallow ocean water, indicating that the shoreline had transgressed even further east. The sandstone at the top of this bed was deposited as sand dunes during a westward regression of the shoreline.

Several other fossils can be found in these sediments in addition to the fossil mollusks. Some of the sediments have sinuous tubes filled with light sand. These were caused by sediment-eating organisms similar to those found along the present shoreline. There are also shells, molds, and siphon tracks of clams and other burrowing bivalves. Rarely, footprints of hoofed mammals have been found in the nonmarine sediments.

This photo shows a layer of light gray bay mud in the Merced Formation that is exposed in the bluff below the Viewing Platform. The small white flakes are fossil sea shells that were deposited in the bay mud about 500,000 years ago. Note the pencil for scale.

In the middle of the bluff below the Viewing Platform there is a layer of white volcanic ash about one foot thick. This ash bed dips north and can be found in the bluff just above the Daly City sewer outlet. This ash layer was deposited in the Merced Formation following a violent eruption of Lassen Peak 400,000 years ago. The ash layer was deposited while this part of the Merced Formation was above sea level. From the amount of ash, it is thought that the eruption was at least as large as the one responsible for the Mazama ash from Crater Lake, Oregon.

The sedimentary layers of the Merced Formation that are exposed along the bluff are mostly tilted to the north. These sediments were horizontal when deposited. The oldest sediments, which are located at the base of the Merced Formation near Mussel Rock, were once buried at a depth of one mile. Following deposition, the sediments were uplifted. The sediments near Mussel Rock have been uplifted about one mile, and tilted to the north. The sediments near Lake Merced have been uplifted only a few hundred feet. The part of the Merced Formation that was uplifted above sea level was subjected to erosion. Because of the tilting, the exposed rocks become progressively older to the south and provide a cross section of the many different layers of rocks that make up the Merced Formation.

By analysis of these rock layers, we know that the sedimentary rocks of the Merced Formation were deposited during Pleistocene time in a small sedimentary basin that had formed in a low spot along the San Andreas fault. Sediments accumulated in this basin because the floor of the basin was continually subsiding, probably because of movement along the San Andreas fault. The sediments were brought to the basin by the Sacramento River system before San Francisco Bay was formed. Eventually, a thickness of about one mile of sediments accumulated in this basin. While the Merced Formation was being deposited, the San Andreas fault was still active. The fault cut the basin into two pieces and moved the pieces apart. The sediments at Fort Funston represent the part of the Merced Formation that was deposited on the east side of the San Andreas fault. The part of the Merced Formation that was deposited on the west side of the fault has been carried slowly northward over the last million years. The town of Bolinas is built on these rocks, and the rocks and the town are still moving north away from Fort Funston.

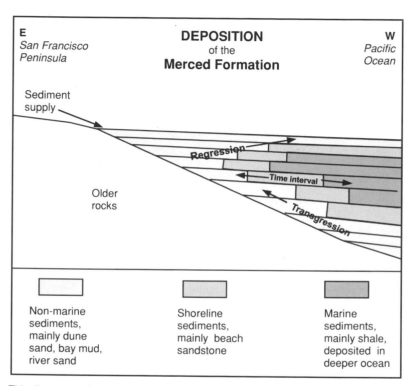

This diagrammatic cross section shows how the Merced Formation was deposited. The rocks consist of many alternating layers of sandstone and shale. Each layer represents sediments deposited during a specific interval of time, and consists of nonmarine sediments to the east, marine sediments to the west, and shoreline sediments inbetween. As the basin subsided, a new layer of sediments was deposited on top of the previous layer. If the basin subsided rapidly, the shoreline *transgressed* landward. If the basin subsided slowly, the shoreline *regressed* seaward. The many layers, or beds, that make up the Merced Formation record the many transgressions and regressions of the shoreline.

Sedimentary Basins in the Coast Ranges

The Merced Formation was deposited in one of the smallest and youngest of many sedimentary basins that were formed in the Coast Ranges during late Cretaceous and early Tertiary time. The first of these sedimentary basins began to form as the Franciscan subduction zone became inactive toward the end of Cretaceous time and the Franciscan rocks were uplifted. This uplift continued throughout Tertiary time and is still in progress. As parts of the Coast Ranges were uplifted, other parts subsided below sea level. The uplifted areas were eroded, and the eroded sediments accumulated in the sedimentary basins. The locations of the uplifts and of the basins changed over time, so that some of the uplifted areas later became basins and some of the basins were later uplifted. The basins were mostly filled with sandstone, shale, siltstone and conglomerate. The type of sediment depended on rates of uplift and deposition, the climate, and the types of sediments being supplied to the basins.

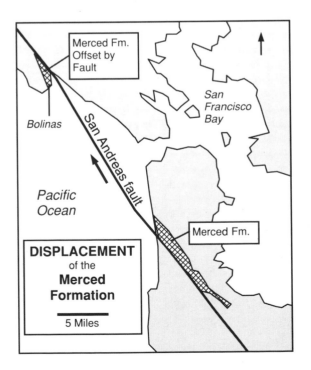

After deposition, the Merced Formation was cut by the San Andreas fault and the rocks on the west side of the fault were carried 20 miles to the north. These rocks are now exposed in the cliffs near Bolinas (see Bolinas Bluff, Trip 7.)

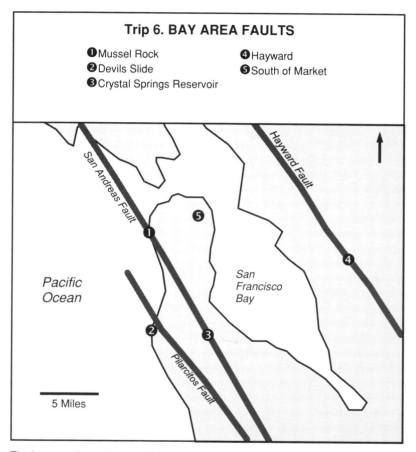

Trip 6. BAY AREA FAULTS

❶ Mussel Rock
❷ Devils Slide
❸ Crystal Springs Reservoir
❹ Hayward
❺ South of Market

The bay area is cut by several large faults that are part of the San Andreas fault system. Two of these faults - the San Andreas and Hayward - are very active and have had a number of major earthquakes over the last 150 years. On the trip to the bay area faults you will investigate these faults and see how they affect roads, houses and buildings in the Bay Area.

Trip 6.
BAY AREA FAULTS
Living with Some Big Faults

During this trip you will see the San Andreas and Hayward faults, two of the largest and most active faults in the San Andreas fault system. The trip involves a 70-mile drive and several short walks, and should take about a day if you go at a leisurely pace. You will visit these localities:

<u>Mussel Rock:</u> The San Andreas fault enters the Pacific at Mussel Rock after a 500-mile journey across southern and central California. On the face of the bluff near Mussel Rock there is a massive landslide formed from crushed rocks of the Merced Formation caught up in the fault zone.

<u>Devils Slide:</u> At Devils Slide, Highway 1 travels high along the face of a steep sea cliff that is cut by a large landslide that periodically closes the highway. The slide occurs in weak rocks along the contact zone between Paleocene sedimentary rocks to the north and a large block of granite to the south that makes up most of Montara Mountain.

<u>Crystal Springs Reservoir:</u> The Crystal Springs and San Andreas Reservoirs lie in a linear valley carved out along the San Andreas fault. Here you will see where the fault that was formed during the 1906 San Francisco earthquake cut through these reservoirs.

<u>Hayward:</u> The Hayward fault cuts through downtown Hayward. In Hayward, you will see a fault scarp near Prospect Street, and where a curb on D Street is being slowly offset by creep along the Hayward fault. You will also drive along Mission Blvd. from Hayward to Fremont and see where recent fault scarps are covered by houses and roads.

<u>South of Market:</u> The area south of Market Street was heavily damaged in the 1906 San Francisco Earthquake and again in the 1989 Loma Prieta Earthquake, largely because the area is underlain by thick unconsolidated water-saturated sediments that shake violently during earthquakes. On the trip to this area you will see places where streets and buildings are slowly sinking because of compaction of these soft sediments.

Mussel Rock

After a 500-mile trip from the Gulf of California and through south and central California, the San Andreas fault leaves the California coast at Mussel Rock and enters the Pacific Ocean. As it leaves the coast, it leaves behind a geological disaster area and a good lesson on how not to use land that is geologically unstable. Several geologic phenomena occur in this area, and all are bad: the area is in a major active fault zone; the rocks in the fault zone are loose and unstable; and the bluff is steep and high. The steep, unstable rocks have caused a major landslide in the bluff. Because of the landslide, the edge of the bluff is rapidly receding, at a rate of up to three feet per year. Land slippage is accelerated when the ground is wet from heavy winter rains. Many houses built at the top of the bluff have been threatened by the landslide and several have been removed as the bluff has receded.

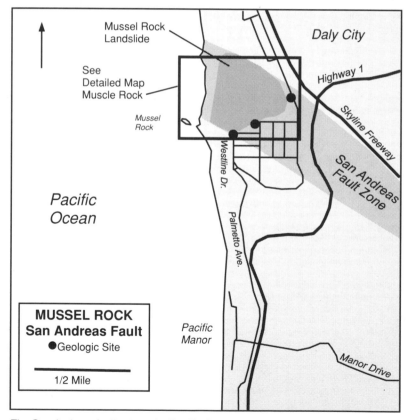

The San Andreas fault enters the Pacific Ocean immediately north of Mussel rock. The landslide in face of the bluff is caused by the weak rocks in the fault zone.

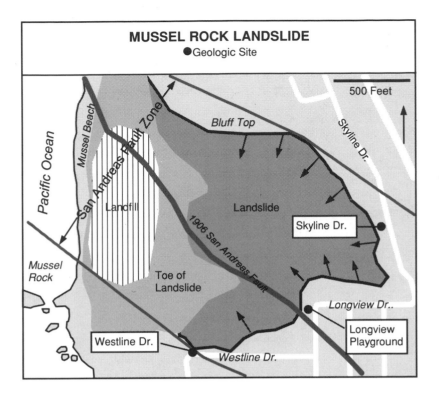

MUSSEL ROCK LANDSLIDE
●Geologic Site

Mussel Rock consists of Franciscan rocks and lies at the south side of the San Andreas fault zone. The fault zone extends from Mussel Rock northward for about one-half mile and includes most of the reentrant in the bluff north of Mussel Rock. The rocks in the fault zone are mainly crushed soft sandstones and shales of the Merced Formation, and it is these rocks that have slumped to form the large landslide that occupies the reentrant. The steep face of the bluff immediately north of the landslide represents the north side of the fault zone.

This area has had several land uses over the last century. From 1905 to 1920, the Ocean Shores Railroad had a rail line along the coastline near the toe of the landslide. The rail line was partly destroyed during the 1906 earthquake and had numerous problems with landslides at many other times. The Coastal Highway was opened in 1936 and followed the old rail line along the coast. This highway also had serious problems with landslides and was finally abandoned in 1957 after an M5.3 earthquake that had its epicenter near Mussel Rock. In the early 1960's, the area along the top of the bluff came under development and many houses were built precariously at the edge of the unstable bluff. From 1963 to 1979, a sanitary landfill was operated in the depression at the base of the landslide. After the sanitary landfill was abandoned, the area of the landfill continued to be used as a dumpsite for construction materials.

Three geologic sites will be visited at Mussel Rock. The first site, on Westline Drive, is at the edge of the bluff overlooking the landslide. Here you'll see cracks along Westline Drive caused by landslides in the unstable rocks at the top of the bluff. The second site, the Longview Playground, is near the fault that was formed during the 1906 San Francisco Earthquake. The third site, on Skyline Drive, is in the San Andreas fault zone and overlooks the landslide scarp formed by the fault zone.

● Westline Drive

To get to this site, follow Highway 1 south from San Francisco to Daly City. Continue on Highway 1 through Daly City. Take the Manor Drive exit 1.5 miles south of the Highway 1 - Highway 35 interchange. Go north on Palmetto Ave. to Westline Drive then follow Westline Drive to the north. Park where Westline Drive turns sharply east at the edge of the bluff.

At the bend in Westline Drive you are at the top of the bluff and near the south edge of the San Andreas fault zone. Several homes at the edge of the bluff in this area have been removed and others are seriously threatened as the bluff has receded because of the landslide. You can see evidence of the land slippage in the arc-shaped cracks in the street and sidewalk along the bend in Westline Drive. These cracks indicate active slumping of the edge of the bluff. From here you also get a good view of the landslide along the face of the bluff to the north.

● Longview Playground

Continue east on Westline Drive one block to Longview Drive, then follow Longview Drive one-half block to the Longview Playground. The Longview Playground is at the south side of the San Andreas fault zone and at the edge of the bluff overlooking the landslide in the bluff. The fault zone consists of hundreds of offsets along the San Andreas fault. The most recent of these offsets was caused by the 1906 San Francisco Earthquake. The trace of the 1906 fault crosses Longview Drive 100 feet south of the playground and then goes through the southwest corner of the playground and continues northwest down the landslide scarp just to the north of the steep gully below the playground.

This photo is taken from the bend in Westline Drive and looks northeast across the reentrant in the bluff formed by the San Andreas fault zone. The road is at the south edge of the fault zone and the opposite cliff is the northeast boundary of the fault zone. The road at this location is close to the edge of the bluff and the arcuate cracks in the road show that this bluff top is slipping downslope.

The trace then crosses the north end of the landfill and goes into the ocean about 500 feet north of the landfill. There is little evidence of the trace of the fault now, since it is largely covered by houses, roads, landfill and beach sand.

●Skyline Drive
From the Longview Playground continue east on Longview Drive three blocks to Skyline Drive, turn north, go 0.1 miles and park. This part of Skyline Drive lies within the San Andreas fault zone and is at the top of the bluff along the steep part of the scarp caused by the landslide. The houses along the cliff here were mostly built from 20 to 40 years ago. Several houses have been removed because of land slippage and several others are threatened. Photos have shown there was twenty feet of cliff erosion in this area from 1979 to 1986.

Devils Slide

The Devils Slide area gets its name from the Devils Slide promontory on the coast about three miles south of Pacifica. There is a large scoop-shaped area on the north side of the promontory that early travelers thought would make a suitable slide for plunging the Devil into the Pacific. Immediately south of this promontory, Highway 1 is precariously cut into the face of a steep cliff about 500 feet above the ocean. A portion of the highway, about 1000 feet long, is built on weak rocks that have formed a landslide. This landslide has the disturbing habit of carrying portions of Highway 1 down the hillside after heavy rainstorms. Even before Highway 1 was built in 1937, these landslides caused much grief to the Ocean Shore Railroad when it ran a rail line through the Devils Slide area from 1908 to 1920. The tracks were removed in 1920 because of high maintenance costs, the constant landslides and other financial problems.

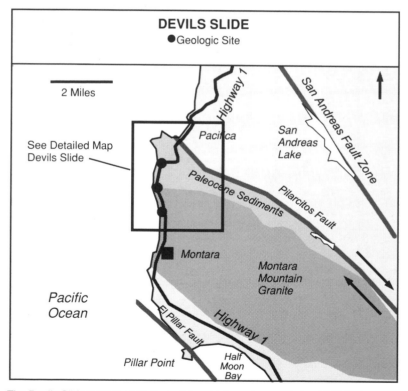

The Devils Slide section of Highway 1 is cut into a steep cliff about 500 feet above sea level for about one mile along the Pacific coastline. Part of the cliff is made up of a major landslide that periodically causes part of Highway 1 to slip toward the Pacific.

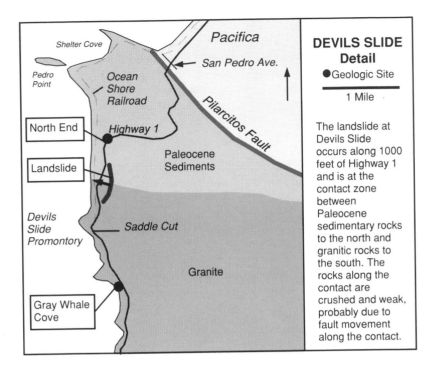

DEVILS SLIDE
Detail
● Geologic Site

1 Mile

The landslide at Devils Slide occurs along 1000 feet of Highway 1 and is at the contact zone between Paleocene sedimentary rocks to the north and granitic rocks to the south. The rocks along the contact are crushed and weak, probably due to fault movement along the contact.

The rocks at the north end of the landslide are severely folded and faulted sandstone and shale of Paleocene age, whereas the rocks at the south end of the landslide, including the Devils Slide promontory, are part of the Montara Mountain granite. The landslide occurs along the contact zone between the Paleocene sedimentary rocks and the granite. The landslides occur because the rocks in the landslide zone are very weak, because there is a steep slope along the shoreline, and because the base of the sea cliff is being constantly removed by marine erosion. As the base of the cliff is removed, the cliff face becomes oversteepened, the weak rocks in the cliff become unstable, and another landslide occurs. After each landslide this entire process starts again.

From detailed studies of Devils Slide area, it appears that the entire cliff, which is 1000 feet high, may be ready to slide into the Pacific. The slide would occur along a slippage surface that is about 300 feet back from the face of the cliff and extends from the top of the cliff to sea level. The slippage surface can be seen at the top of the cliff as a steep scarp about 30 feet high and over 1000 feet long.

On the trip to Devils Slide you will see three geologic sites. At the north end of the landslide, you will see the Paleocene sedimentary rocks that make up the north part of the landslide. The second site is a drive along the landslide. Because this part of Highway 1 is narrow and unstable, you may not be permitted to park, but you can see the rocks in the landslide as you drive by. The third site is at Gray Whale Cove State Beach where you will see the granitic rocks that make up the south part of the landslide.

The Devils Slide section of Highway 1 is particularly susceptible to sliding in the winter after heavy winter rains. The rains saturate the weak rocks in the slide area and these rocks begin to move downslope. These landslides have been responsible for closing Highway 1 for many days, and in some cases for weeks. Because of the problems with closures and the high cost of road maintenance, an alternate 4.5 mile route has been proposed that would be built one mile inland and bypass Devils Slide. This alternate route is highly controversial since it would cut through McNee Ranch State Park and would require extensive tunneling and deep road cuts that would cause many ecological and environmental problems.

This photograph, from the north end of Devils Slide, shows the steeply dipping layers of Paleocene sedimentary rocks that form Pedro Point. The abandoned roadbed of the Ocean Shore Railroad can be seen sloping down the cliff toward the point.

● *North End*

The trip to Devils Slide starts in Pacifica at the intersection of Highway 1 and San Pedro Ave. Set your odometer at 0.0 miles at this intersection. Going south from this intersection, Highway 1 leaves the coast and climbs into the hills. These hills were formed by uplift along the Pilarcitos fault. Although there has been little or no movement on the Pilarcitos fault over the last million years, it was at one time very active, and still leaves its mark on the landscape. The Pilarcitos fault follows the San Pedro Valley to the southeast, then continues through Pilarcitos Lake and joins the San Andreas fault just west of Stanford University. The San Pedro Valley and Pilarcitos Lake were eroded in the fractured rocks along the fault zone.

As you drive to the first stop you will pass several road cuts of thinly layered sandstone and shale of Paleocene age. At 1.2 miles Highway 1 returns to the coast and immediately on the right there is a pullout with a large metal equipment cage. Park in this pullout. At this locality you are at the north end of Devil's Slide and the Highway is 465 feet above sea level. The Paleocene sedimentary rocks are well exposed in the road cut behind you. These rocks were originally deposited in southern California about 60 million years ago and have been carried north to their present

This photograph shows the Paleocene sedimentary rocks at the north end of Devils Slide. The rocks consist of interbedded sandstone and shale and dip steeply to the north.

position by the Pilarcitos and San Andreas faults. The rocks are mainly sandstone and shale, but siltstone and conglomerate also occur. Some of the conglomerates have cobbles of granite similar to the Montara Mountain granite, indicating that they were derived from erosion of the granite. The Paleocene rocks are steeply tilted to the northwest, and in some outcrops the beds are also bent into small folds. These folds formed when the soft sedimentary rocks in the vicinity of the Pilarcitos fault were squeezed by the fault movement as they were carried north on the west side of the fault.

Looking north from the pullout you can see Pedro Point. The Paleocene sedimentary rocks are exposed along the cliff face from the pullout to and including Pedro Point. The Ocean Shore Railroad followed the coast around Pedro Point, and you can still see the rail bed gently cutting down the face of the cliff toward Pedro Point.

During the last 10,000 years the bluff you are standing on extended several tens of miles further west. As sea level rose after the last glacial period, the bluff has eroded eastward to its present position, and the bluff is still being eroded to the east.

●Landslide

Continue driving south on Highway 1. At 1.6 miles you will reach the landslide and you will be in the landslide for the next thousand feet. You may not be able to stop or park on this section of the highway, but you can observe the rocks in the road cuts as you drive by. Note that the Paleocene rocks at the north end of the landslide are highly contorted and mashed. At about the middle of the landslide you cross the contact between these contorted Paleocene sedimentary rocks and the granite. The granitic rocks along this contact zone are also crushed and weak. As you continue south past the landslide, note that the granite is quite different from the Paleocene sediments. There is no bedding in the granite. South of the landslide the granite weathers into large blocks that are yellow-brown in color.

At 1.8 miles you will pass through a very steep road-cut in the granite called the Saddle Cut. Devils Slide promontory, also granite, juts out into the Pacific to the west of this cut. The old rail line along the coast to Pacifica went through Saddle Cut. The rocks from Saddle Cut to Gray Whale Cove State Beach are all granite. The next stop will be the parking area for the State Beach.

●*Gray Whale Cove*

At 2.8 miles pull into the unmarked parking area on the left for Gray Whale Cove State Beach. The rocks in the parking area and in the small hill just north of the parking area are granite. This granite extends from the landslide at Devils Slide south through Montara and makes up all of Montara Mountain. The granite is massive, without layering, but tends to form large blocks as it weathers. Where it is weathered in the parking area and in road cuts, the granite is colored yellow-brown, but is light gray where it is fresh and not weathered.

If you look at the granite in detail you will see that it is composed of many sharp grains about the size of a small pea. Most of the grains are light colored, but about 20% are black. The light-colored grains are quartz and feldspar, and the black grains are biotite and hornblende. For a more detailed description of the granite and how the granite was formed, see the discussion of the granite at the Point Reyes Headlands on the trip to the Point Reyes Peninsula.

If you wish to see fresh exposures of the granite, take the trail to Gray Whale Cove State Beach. However, be forewarned that this is a clothing-optional beach and you may see much more than just granite. Alternately, you will see more weathered granite in the road cuts along Highway 1 to Montara.

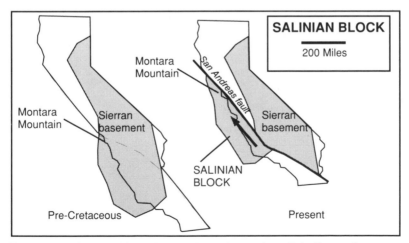

The granite at Montara Mountain is similar to the granite at Point Reyes, the Farallon Islands, Bodega Head, and in the Santa Lucia Range. All of this granite is part of a large basement block called the Salinian block. The Salinian block was cut off from the southern Sierras by the San Andreas fault and has been slowly moving northward over the last 25 million years.

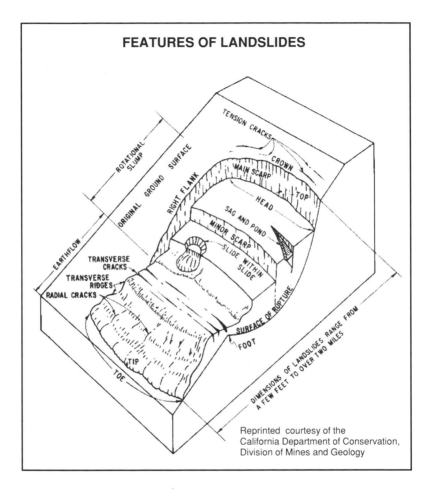

FEATURES OF LANDSLIDES

Reprinted courtesy of the
California Department of Conservation,
Division of Mines and Geology

Landslides

There are many landslides in the Coast Ranges of northern California, where slopes are steep, rocks are weak, and there is high rainfall. A typical landslide has a number of characteristic features that are usually formed as a result of the slide. There is usually a steep scarp shaped like an amphitheater at the top of the slide. This scarp is the exposed portion of the rupture surface along which the rocks are sliding. The rupture surface is shaped like a scoop. The lower part of the scoop comes out on the surface further downslope, where it is called the *toe* of the landslide. The rocks within the slide tend to form rotated blocks. The rocks below the toe have flowed downslope and tend to form arcuate bulbous transverse ridges. Depending on the type of rocks in the landslide and the amount of water in the rocks, the movement of the slide can be rapid, in feet per minute, or slow, in inches per day or week. With time, erosion modifies the landslide features so that it is difficult to identify older inactive landslides. Many hillsides in the Coast Ranges consist of multiple landslide scars in different degrees of weathering, resulting in an irregular lumpy appearance.

In addition to steep slopes and weak rocks there are several other factors that may contribute to landslides. Heavy rainfall over a long period of time can increase the moisture content of the rocks on the hillside and reduce the strength of the rocks. Earthquakes may also trigger landslides. The large 1906 San Francisco Earthquake caused numerous landslides in the vicinity of the fault. Man-made cuts for roads or other construction may remove support from the toe of slopes, thereby contributing to landslides. Septic systems can add to the moisture to the soil, weakening the strength of the rocks.

Many houses and buildings in northern California are built on land subject to landslides. If you own a house in California that is on or near a steep slope, consider having the location checked by a certified geologist or engineer.

Crystal Springs Reservoir

The Crystal Springs Reservoir lies within the San Andreas fault zone. On this trip you'll see many of the topographic features that are characteristic of the fault zone. During the Great San Francisco Earthquake of 1906, the active trace of the San Andreas fault cut through the Crystal Springs Reservoir, San Andreas Lake, and through the stream valley between the lake and the reservoir. This is one of the few places near San Francisco where the trace of the 1906 earthquake can still be seen. In most other places near San Francisco the fault has been covered over by roads and buildings.

On the trip to the Crystal Springs Reservoir you will visit two geologic sites that were affected by the San Andreas fault during the 1906 earthquake. The first site is the causeway that crosses Crystal Springs Reservoir. The old causeway across the reservoir was offset eight feet during the 1906 earthquake. At the second site, the San Andreas Dam, you will see where the east abutment of the dam was offset nine feet during the 1906 earthquake.

The San Andreas fault has affected the topography in many places along its 750-mile journey from the Gulf of California to Cape Mendocino on the northern California coast. The fault zone is typically about half-a-mile wide. Within the fault zone there are many old fault breaks that were made at different times by movement along the fault. These fault breaks are separated by blocks of more competent rocks that form linear ridges and linear troughs. Some of the linear ridges have steep scarps from recent faulting. Some of the fault troughs have no drainage and therefore form lakes called *sag ponds*. The Crystal Springs Reservoir and San Andreas Lake are like large sag ponds in the fault zone, but they have been enhanced by the Crystal Springs and San Andreas dams.

The Crystal Springs Reservoir supplies water to San Francisco and many other peninsular towns. Most of the water comes from Hetch Hetchy Valley in the Sierras. The Crystal Springs Dam was completed in 1888, and was then one of the largest concrete dams in the world. The foundation of the dam is in fractured Franciscan graywackes. Despite this uncertain foundation, the dam had no damage during the 1906 earthquake, even though the fault offset was in the lake only 1000 feet west of the dam.

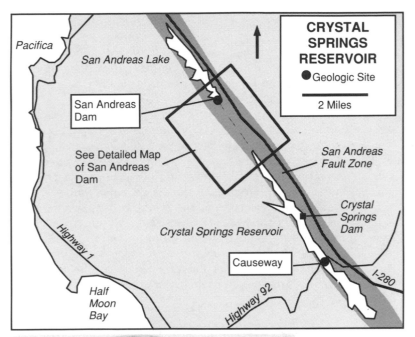

This air photo looks northwest along the Crystal Springs Reservoir. The reservoir lies in an elongated valley formed along the San Andreas fault zone. The causeway can be seen in the upper part of the photo. (From Wallace, 1990)

●*Causeway*

To reach the Crystal Springs Reservoir from Devils Slide, go south on Highway 1 to Highway 92 at Half Moon Bay, then go east 6.8 miles on Highway 92 to the Crystal Springs Reservoir. You will not be able to stop on the causeway, so continue east across the causeway, stay right on Highway 92 and pull over into the first parking area. From here you can get a good view of the causeway and the reservoir.

The causeway that takes Highway 92 across the Crystal Springs Reservoir crosses the most recent trace of the San Andreas fault. During the 1906 San Francisco Earthquake the old causeway across the reservoir was offset eight feet, with the west side going north. The new causeway crosses the reservoir at the same place, but unfortunately the new causeway was straightened out and all traces of the earlier fault movement have been obliterated. The causeway was just one of many places where roads, fences, and stream valleys were offset during the 1906 fault, always with the west side moving north. From this viewpoint you can look north and south along the reservoir and see the northwest-trending linear valley that was formed along the San Andreas fault zone.

The old causeway across the Crystal Springs Reservoir was offset eight feet to the north during the 1906 San Francisco Earthquake, as can be seen in this photo. (Photograph courtesy of Branner Library, Stanford University)

●San Andreas Dam

To reach the San Andreas Dam from the causeway, continue east on Highway 92, then turn north on I-280. Go north 6.5 miles on I-280 then take the Millbrae Avenue exit. Do not turn on Millbrae Avenue, but continue north to Hillcrest Blvd. Go west on Hillcrest Blvd. under I-280 to the trailhead for the Sawyer Camp Trail. Follow the trail to the dam. This is a hike of about 1.0 mile round trip and will take about one hour. Allow another hour and a half if you wish to continue south from the dam on the Sawyer Camp Trail to see some other features along the trace of the 1906 fault.

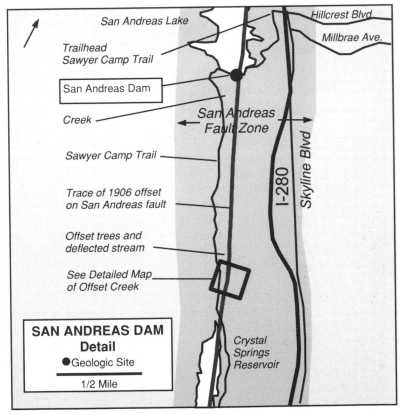

The trace of the 1906 San Francisco Earthquake cut the embankment immediately adjacent to the east side of the San Andreas dam. South of the dam, along the Sawyer Camp Trail, fences, rows of trees and small creeks were offset by the fault. The detailed map shows offset of one of these creeks.

Air photo of San Andreas Lake, looking northwest. The line indicates the approximate trace of the 1906 earthquake. (Reprinted courtesy of the California Department of Conservation, Division of Mines and Geology)

The San Andreas Dam is an earthfill embankment that is 720 feet long and was built across the valley that was formed by the San Andreas fault zone. The original dam was completed in 1870, and then raised in 1875 and again in 1928. The trace of the 1906 earthquake did not cut the earthfill dam, but cut through the ridge that forms the abutment immediately east of the dam. The dam was displaced nine feet to the northwest during the earthquake, but did not fail. From the east abutment of the dam, the fault goes into San Andreas Lake, and then closely follows along the eastern shore of the lake. It is this lake that gave its name to the San Andreas fault. In 1991 a monument was placed at the spot where the fault cut through the abutment.

Sawyer Camp Trail: If you have time, you may wish to continue south from the dam along the Sawyer Camp Trail for another 1.6 miles. The trail lies immediately west of the trace of the 1906 San Francisco fault. Along the trail there are many topographic features that were formed or altered during the 1906 earthquake and by numerous earlier earthquakes along the fault. About 1.5 miles south of the San Andreas Dam there is a fence and row of cypress trees that were offset nine feet during the 1906 earthquake. A little further south, there is a stream that has been offset about 200 feet during the 1906 earthquake and several earlier earthquakes. This 200-foot offset would represent at least 20 earthquakes of the magnitude of the 1906 earthquake.

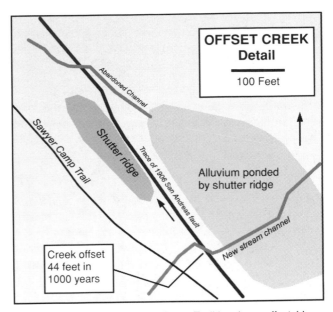

A small creek near the Sawyer Camp Trail has been offset 44 feet during the last 1000 years by a recent trace of the San Andreas fault.

At 1.6 miles south of the San Andreas Dam, just before the trail crosses the creek between San Andreas Lake and the Crystal Springs Reservoir, there is a small creek that has been offset 44 feet by the fault. Detailed studies using radiocarbon dating suggest that this offset occurred during the last 1000 years, an average rate of about one-half inch per year. According to this study, a small stream flowed across the San Andreas fault in this area several thousand years ago. The old abandoned stream channel north of the ponded alluvium is a remnant of this early drainage. Following a major earthquake, a shutter ridge formed along the west side of the fault. The shutter ridge blocked the old stream channel and formed a pond on the east side of the fault. Continued movement along the fault carried the shutter ridge north until finally the shutter ridge was out of the way and a new stream channel was cut across the fault. The pond was drained when the new channel was cut. Radioactive dating shows that the pond dried up 1000 years ago. When the new stream channel was formed 1000 years ago, it flowed directly across the fault trace. During the last 1000 years, this channel has been offset 44 feet by several movements of the fault, including the movement in 1906.

Hayward

The Hayward fault is over 60 miles long and trends northwest from San Jose through Fremont, Hayward, Oakland, Berkeley, and Richmond into San Pablo Bay. This is a heavily populated area and many buildings and houses have been built directly on the fault. This trip will begin at Hayward with a nine-mile drive along the fault following Mission Blvd. from Hayward south to Fremont. On this drive you will see some of the topographic features caused by the Hayward fault. You will then return to downtown Hayward to see the Hayward fault at D Street and on Prospect Street.

The Hayward fault is one of the most active faults in the entire San Andreas fault system. Some of the movement along the fault has been by slow creep. The land on the west side of the fault is creeping north at a rate of about 0.2"/year relative to the land on the east side of the fault. In places, buildings have been built across the fault and the fault is slowly tearing the buildings apart. The Old Court House in Hayward lies directly over the fault, as does the stadium at the University of California at Berkeley. In five million years the west half of the Old Court House in Hayward will adjoin the east half of the stadium at Berkeley. If you waited in the court house long enough you could see half of the Berkeley-Stanford football game from your chair in the court house.

In addition to the creep along the fault, there have also been several major earthquakes on the Hayward fault, accompanied by offsets of a couple of feet or so. In 1836 there was a M6.8 earthquake north of San Leandro; in 1858 there was a M6.3 earthquake near San Jose; and in 1868 there was a M7.0 earthquake near Hayward.

During the 1868 Hayward Earthquake the earth was ruptured for a distance of 35 miles, from Berkeley to Warm Springs near the Santa Clara line. Maximum reported offset was three feet with a slight down-throw on the southwest side. Nearly every house in the town of Hayward was thrown off its foundation and many buildings were destroyed. On page 162 of this book there is an eyewitness account of the effects of this earthquake on downtown Hayward.

Shortly after the earthquake, a committee of scientific men made an investigation of the fault, but their report was never published. Indications are that the report was suppressed by authorities through fear that its publication would damage the reputation of the city.

There have been several attempts to predict the probability of future earthquakes along the Hayward fault. In 1988, the U.S. Geological Survey estimated that there was a 20% probability of a M6.5 to M7.0 event in the interval from 1988 to 2018. A 1996 report by the Association of Bay Area Governments ups the chances to one in three that the Bay Area will have a major shock in the next ten years. Some seismologists think that this earthquake could be as large as M7.5.

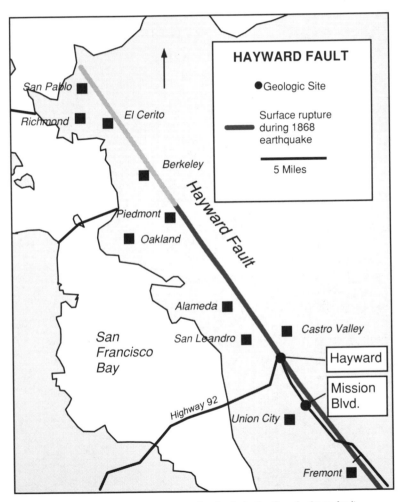

The Hayward fault, one of the most active faults in the San Andreas fault system, goes through many communities in the East Bay. These communities are at high risk for major damage in the event of a large earthquake on the fault.

●*Mission Blvd.*

To get to Mission Blvd. from the Crystal Springs Reservoir, continue east on Highway 92 across San Francisco Bay to Hayward, then turn right on Mission Blvd. The drive along Mission Blvd. starts at the intersection of Highway 92 and Mission Blvd. Set your odometer at 0.0 miles at this intersection. From here you will drive south on Mission Blvd. toward Fremont.

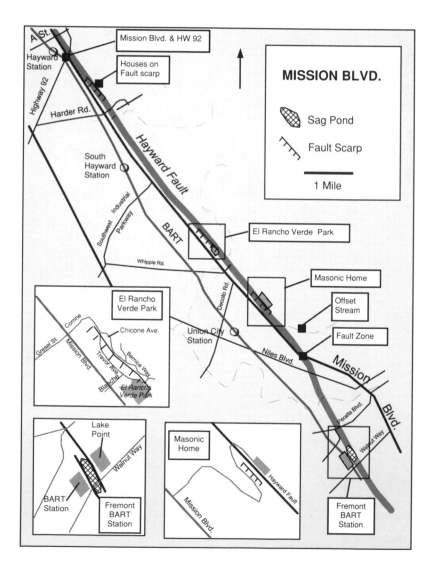

0.0 Miles, Mission Blvd. & HW 92: This intersection is in the fault zone of the Hayward fault. The fault zone is about 0.25 miles wide and consists of many fault traces from earlier faults and earthquakes. The fault zone is paved over in this intersection, so don't expect to see any indications of the fault.

1.0 Miles, Houses on Fault Scarp: On your left, note the rows of houses built on the top of a steep cliff. The cliff is a fault scarp. A recent trace of the Hayward fault lies near the base of the scarp.

3.3 Miles, El Rancho Verde Park: Note the houses built on the top of the fault scarp above El Rancho Verde Park. You can take a short loop and drive up the fault scarp and along the top of the scarp. See the detailed map on the opposite page. Bernice Way is on the top of the fault scarp and Trevor Avenue is at the base of the scarp.

5.3 Miles, Masonic Home: The most recently active strand of the Hayward fault lies at the foot of the slope in front of the Masonic Home. There was movement on this strand of the fault in 1868.

6.1 Miles, Offset Stream: As you enter Fremont, look on the hill ahead and to your left. You will see a stream valley that has been offset by the Hayward fault. There are many other similar offset streams along the fault zone.

7.0 Miles, Fault Zone: Mission Blvd. bends to the east. At this point you are crossing the fault zone. The remainder of the trip will be on the northeast side of the fault until you reach the Fremont BART Station.

8.7 Miles, Fremont BART Station: Turn right from Mission Blvd. onto Walnut Way and go 1.0 mile to the Fremont BART Station. The Hayward fault is immediately east of the BART Station. There is a small sag pond in the fault zone between the station and the Lake Point development on Walnut Way.

The next two geologic sites are in downtown Hayward, so retrace your route along Mission Blvd. to Hayward. In Hayward, continue north on Mission Blvd. across Highway 92, and then go one block to D Street. Park at Mission Blvd. and D Street.

● *D Street*

The Hayward fault goes directly through downtown Hayward, and there are at least two active traces of the Hayward fault between Mission Blvd. and Main Street. The effects of these faults can be seen on nearly every cross street from D Street to Sunset Blvd. The fault effects include offset curbs, sidewalks, foundations, and cracks in the street.

One of the best places to see fault offset is on D Street between Mission Blvd. and Main Street. Take a walk along this section of D Street and look for offset curbs and other fault features. The curb on D Street has been offset by creep along one of the strands of the Hayward fault. Precise surveys on this curb show that the southwest side of the fault is moving north at an average rate of about 0.1"/year. Other strands of the Hayward fault are also active, so that the total displacement along all strands of the fault in Hayward is about 0.2"/year. Creep along the Hayward fault took a siesta after the 1989 Loma Prieta earthquake, but recent indications are that the creep has resumed.

This curb on D Street in downtown Hayward has been offset by creep along an active segment of the Hayward fault. Precise measurements over a twenty-year period show that the curb is being offset at an average rate of 0.1"/year.

● *Prospect Street*

Another remarkable fault feature in downtown Hayward is a well-defined bedrock ridge that has been uplifted along the Hayward fault. Prospect Street is situated on the top of this ridge and the steep slope between Prospect Street and Mission Blvd. is a fault scarp. To get to Prospect Street from D Street, go north on Mission Blvd. 0.4 miles to Hotel Street. Turn right on Hotel Street and go one block. Turn left on Prospect Street. As you drive north on Prospect Street note the steep drop-off to the east and to the west. Turn left at Rose Street and go back to Mission Blvd. Turn left on Mission Blvd. toward downtown Hayward. As you drive south on Mission Blvd. you will get good views of the very steep fault scarp between Simon and Hotel Streets. The top of the ridge on Prospect Street is about 60 feet higher than the base of the scarp on Mission Blvd.

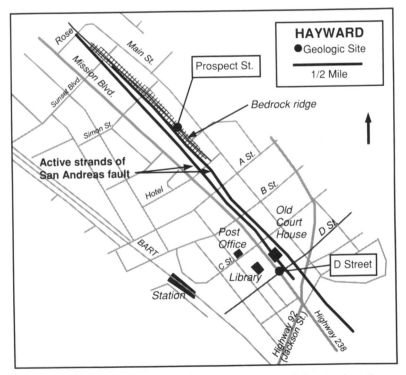

The Hayward fault goes directly through downtown Hayward. Structures on the west side of the fault in Hayward, including the library and post office, are moving north at about 0.2"/year relative to structures on the east side of the fault. Scarps occur along the fault in many places. The bedrock ridge along Prospect Street is along the top of one of these scarps.

South of Market

Although the South of Market area is not on the San Andreas or Hayward faults, it has been especially susceptible to heavy damage during earthquakes because the area is underlain by thick, unconsolidated water-saturated sediments. Shaking is intensified in these loose sediments during major earthquakes. Modified Mercalli Intensity readings for this area during the Great San Francisco Earthquake of 1906 were IX and X, compared to readings of VII and VIII for most of the other parts of the city. This area was again shaken violently during the Loma Prieta Earthquake of 1989, with intensities of VIII and IX compared to VI to VII for most of the city. During the 1989 Loma Prieta Earthquake, liquefaction also occurred in local areas, causing some structures to settle a foot or more. Earthquake damage has been especially severe between Fifth and Eighth Streets and Mission and Townsend Streets. On the geologic trip to this area, you will walk along Clara Street, where you will see how these buildings are slowly subsiding in these loose sediments.

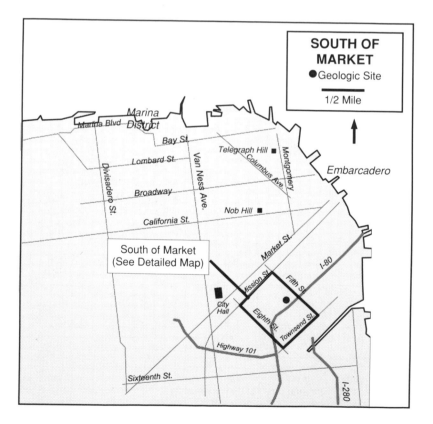

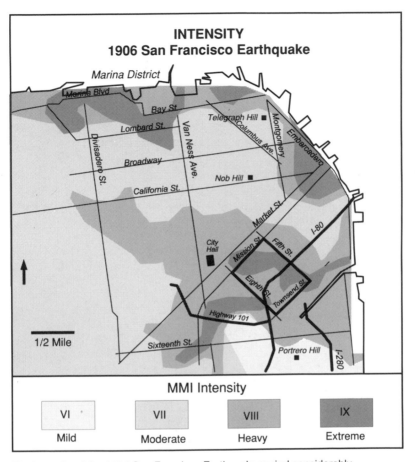

INTENSITY
1906 San Francisco Earthquake

MMI Intensity

VI	VII	VIII	IX
Mild	Moderate	Heavy	Extreme

The intensity of the 1906 San Francisco Earthquake varied considerably throughout San Francisco, depending on whether structures were built on hard rock or on loose unconsolidated sediments. The highest earthquake intensities were recorded in the areas built on loose unconsolidated sediments - the South of Market area, along the Embarcadero, and the Marina District. These areas had the highest earthquake intensities again in the 1989 Loma Prieta Earthquake. The parts of the city built on hard Franciscan rocks felt only mild and moderate shaking during these earthquakes. These areas included Nob Hill and Telegraph Hill, built on hard Alcatraz sandstone, and Portrero Hill, built on a block of hard serpentine in the Hunters Point melange.

● *Clara Street*

To get to Clara Street from Hayward, go north on Jackson Street to Foothill Blvd., continue north on I-580 to I-80, then follow I-80 across the Bay Bridge. In San Francisco, take the Fifth Street exit, go one block past Harrison Street and turn left onto Clara Street.

Most of the buildings along Clara Street are old, but all were built after the 1906 earthquake. The earlier buildings were destroyed in the 1906 fire and earthquake. As you walk along Clara Street, look for the following:

1. Side alleys and side yards that are several feet lower than the street. Main roads and utility lines were periodically raised to grade, whereas the buildings, yards and side alleys continued to subside.

2. Houses where the original entrance is below street grade. In these houses, short steps now lead up several feet to an entrance on the second

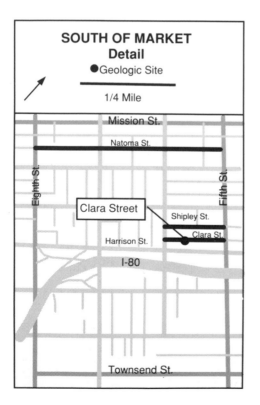

SOUTH OF MARKET Detail

● Geologic Site

1/4 Mile

Mission St.

Natoma St.

Eighth St.

Fifth St.

Clara Street

Shipley St.

Harrison St.

Clara St.

I-80

Townsend St.

Many of the buildings on Clara Street have subsided several feet because of compaction of the loose unconsolidated sediments that underlie this part of the city. As the buildings subsided, Clara Street has been built up to maintain the original elevation. Thus, the side yards and entrances to the buildings are now several feet below grade.

floor. The first floor is the basement. This architectural problem occurred when the street level was brought up to grade, yet the front entrance to the house remained several feet below grade.

3. Leaning buildings, caused by uneven subsidence.

Other good places to see similar subsidence features are Shipley Street from Fifth Street to Sixth Street, and Natoma Street from Fifth Street to Eighth Street.

This building on Clara Street shows the effects of subsidence due to the thick soft sediments in the South of Market area. The building has subsided several feet. The sidewalk and street have been built up to maintain the original grade level of the street. The top of the garage door is at waist level. The entrance door to the house has been repositioned to enter the house at mid-level. The window on the right was once on the second floor of the house.

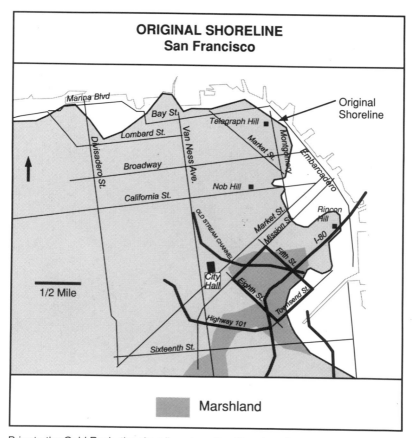

ORIGINAL SHORELINE
San Francisco

Marshland

Prior to the Gold Rush, the shoreline along San Francisco Bay was considerably different from today's shoreline. This original shoreline roughly followed Marina Blvd. and Bay Street, then wrapped around Telegraph Hill and followed Montgomery Street to Market Street. The shoreline then wrapped around Rincon Hill. Much of the area south of Rincon Hill and Market Street was marshland and the marshland extended almost to City Hall. A small stream flowed across the marshland from the Civic Center to Fourth and Bryant Streets where the stream emptied into the bay. The area bounded by Mission, Townsend, Fifth and Eighth Streets is built on this old marshland.

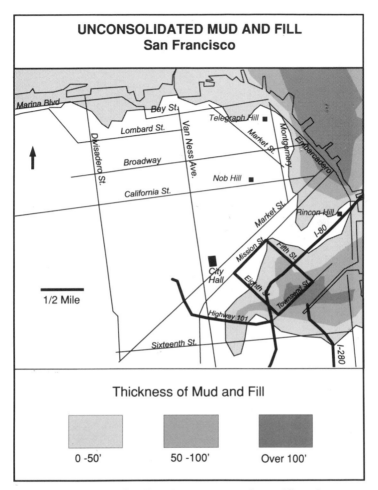

UNCONSOLIDATED MUD AND FILL
San Francisco

1/2 Mile

Thickness of Mud and Fill

0 -50'   50 -100'   Over 100'

During the Gold Rush, San Francisco was expanding rapidly and developers considered the marshland south of Market Street as prime real estate. They filled the marsh with garbage, quarry rubble and dune sand, and proceeded to build. Little did they know, or perhaps care, that they had piled this rubble on top of soft, unconsolidated, water-saturated sediments. In some places, as along Townsend Street, these sediments were over 100-feet thick. Most of the fill in Marina District came later, and was mainly rubble from the 1906 earthquake. This rubble was dumped on soft, unconsolidated sediments along the shoreline, and buildings were constructed on the fill. The 1989 Loma Prieta earthquake showed that this was not a red-hot idea.

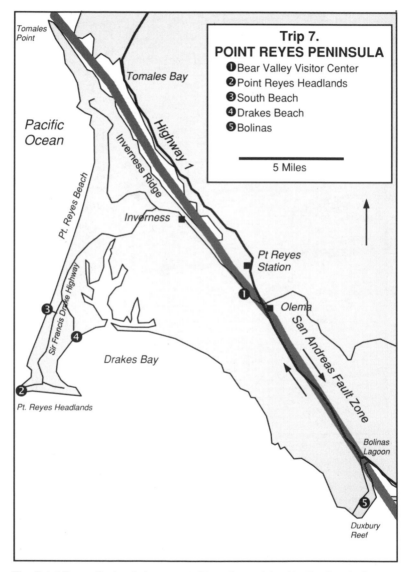

The Point Reyes Peninsula is separated from the mainland by the San Andreas fault. Many of the rocks on the peninsula are from south and central California and have been carried to their present position by movement along the San Andreas fault over the last 25 million years.

Trip 7.
POINT REYES PENINSULA
The Long Trip North

The Point Reyes Peninsula is a piece of southern California that has been carried north by the San Andreas fault several hundred miles during the last 25 million years. As it moved north, the peninsula accumulated rocks from several different places in south and central California and carried these rocks with it, like a tramp steamer adding cargo to its deck. You will see several of these well-traveled rock units during the geologic trip to the Point Reyes Peninsula. It would be best to allow two days for this trip. The Point Reyes Peninsula lies within the Point Reyes National Seashore, and is administered by the National Park Service (Phone 415-663-1092). These are the places you will visit:

Bear Valley Visitor Center: On the Earthquake Trail near the visitor center you will walk along the San Andreas fault zone.

Point Reyes Headlands: At the Point Reyes Headlands you will see the granite that forms the basement rocks that underlie the entire Point Reyes Peninsula. You will also see the Point Reyes Conglomerate that covers the granite and forms the east and west tips of the headlands.

South Beach: This beach has some of the largest waves along the entire California coast. You will see how these waves play a major role in shaping the shoreline of the Point Reyes Peninsula.

Drakes Beach: At Drakes Beach you will see the white cliffs of the Drakes Bay Formation. When Sir Francis Drake was here in 1579 these cliffs reminded him of the white cliffs of Dover.

Bolinas: At the bluff near Bolinas you will see rocks of the Merced Formation that have been carried here from the Fort Funston area by the San Andreas fault. At nearby Agate Beach you will see the Monterey Shale, which covers much of the southern part of the Point Reyes Peninsula. These rocks probably came from the Monterey Bay area.

Geologic Map
The geologic map on the opposite page shows the main rock units that make up the Point Reyes Peninsula. The granite underlies the entire peninsula and is exposed along the Inverness Ridge, at Tomales Point, and at the Point Reyes Headlands. The Point Reyes Conglomerate rests on top of the granite, but is found only at the east and west tips of the Point Reyes Headlands. The Monterey Shale covers most of the southern part of the Point Reyes Peninsula and is well exposed along the coastline south of Drakes Bay to Duxbury Reef. The Drakes Bay Formation covers most of the western part of the Peninsula and is exposed along the cliffs of Drakes Bay. Exposures of the Merced Formation are quite limited, but these rocks can be seen on the west side of the Bolinas Lagoon near the town of Bolinas.

The cross section shows the rocks as they appear at depth under the peninsula. The rocks have been uplifted to form two broad anticlines, one along the Point Reyes Headlands and one along the Inverness Ridge. The Monterey Shale was folded, then partly eroded before deposition of the Drakes Bay Formation.

ROCK UNITS
Point Reyes Peninsula

Locality (Geologic Site)	Rock Unit	Age	Description
Bolinas (Bolinas Bluff)	Merced Formation	Pleistocene	Blue-gray siltstone and soft brown sandstone, very soft.
Drakes Beach	Drakes Bay Formation	Pliocene	Cream-colored siltstone and gray-to-yellow mudstone.
Bolinas (Agate Beach)	Monterey Shale	Miocene	Thinly bedded light-gray shale; breaks into sharp fragments.
Point Reyes Headlands (Lighthouse)	Point Reyes Conglomerate	Paleocene	Very hard conglomerate with boulders of chert, volcanic rocks and granite.
Point Reyes Headlands (Sea Lion Overlook)	Granitic rocks	Cretaceous	Granite, light gray, coarse grained, hard, similar to granite in Sierras.

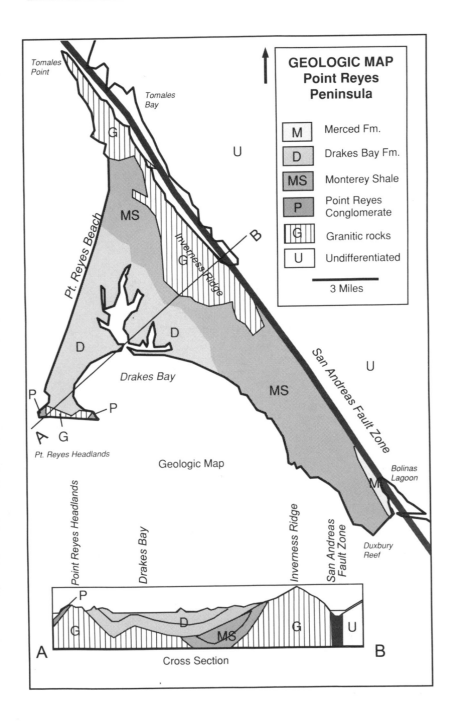

**GEOLOGIC MAP
Point Reyes
Peninsula**

M	Merced Fm.
D	Drakes Bay Fm.
MS	Monterey Shale
P	Point Reyes Conglomerate
G	Granitic rocks
U	Undifferentiated

3 Miles

Tomales Point

Tomales Bay

U

G

Pt. Reyes Beach

MS

Inverness Ridge

G

B

D

D

Drakes Bay

P

P

A G

Pt. Reyes Headlands

Geologic Map

San Andreas Fault Zone

U

MS

M

Bolinas Lagoon

Duxbury Reef

Point Reyes Headlands

Drakes Bay

Inverness Ridge

San Andreas Fault Zone

P

G

D

MS

G

U

A

B

Cross Section

Bear Valley Visitor Center

The Bear Valley visitor center lies within the San Andreas fault zone and provides a good opportunity to look at the fault zone in detail. To reach the visitor center, follow Highway 1 to Olema, then turn west on Bear Valley Road and go 0.7 miles to the visitor center.

The San Andreas fault zone in this area is from one-half to one-mile wide. The rocks within the fault zone have been shattered and weakened by the faulting so they have been eroded to form the broad topographic low that extends from Bolinas Lagoon to Tomales Bay. The fault zone consists of hundreds of smaller faults along which movement has taken place over millions of years. Although most of this movement has been

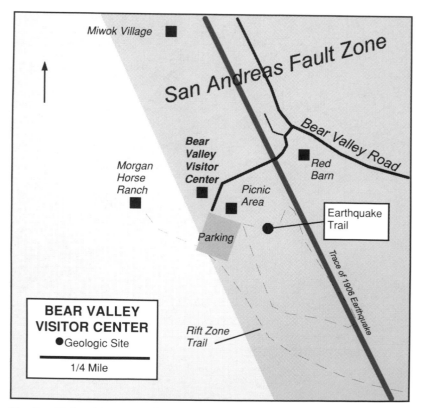

The Bear Valley visitor center lies within the San Andreas fault zone and is near the fault trace of the 1906 San Francisco Earthquake. You will see many of the fault features that are characteristic of transform faults along the Earthquake Trail and the Rift Zone Trail. Both trails leave from the visitor center.

horizontal, there was also some vertical offset. These numerous faults have formed a messy and jumbled topography. Features to look for within the fault zone include linear ridges, small fault scarps, stream drainage that has been offset or disrupted by the fault movement, sag ponds formed in low areas with no outlet, meadows that were once sag ponds but have been filled in, streams separated by linear ridges that flow in opposite directions, and rows of trees that have been offset.

The Bear Valley visitor center lies near one of the faulted linear ridges in the San Andreas fault zone. You can see many more of the topographic features that are characteristic of the fault zone by a short walk along the Earthquake Trail near the visitor center. Other good places to see the fault are along the Rift Zone Trail and along Highway 1 from Olema to the Bolinas Lagoon, where Highway 1 follows the rift zone.

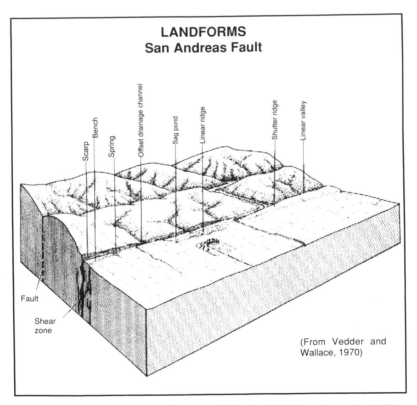

**LANDFORMS
San Andreas Fault**

Scarp Bench Spring Offset drainage channel Sag pond Linear ridge Shutter ridge Linear valley

Fault

Shear zone

(From Vedder and Wallace, 1970)

This diagram shows some of the topographic features that have been formed by the San Andreas fault.

●*Earthquake Trail*

The trailhead for the 0.5-mile Earthquake Trail is east of the visitor center next to the picnic area. This trail has a number of exhibits that explain the San Andreas fault and the Great San Francisco Earthquake of 1906. During this earthquake the ground along the San Andreas fault was fractured for a distance of 270 miles, from San Juan Bautista in the south to Alder Creek in the north, where the fault enters the Pacific. Over this entire distance, fences, roads, railroad tracks, and buildings that crossed the fault trace were offset from a few feet up to 21 feet. In each case, the land on the west side of the fault moved north. The entire Point Reyes Peninsula lurched north about 20 feet relative to the mainland.

The epicenter of the 1906 earthquake was offshore, between Mussel Rock and the Point Reyes Peninsula. The largest recorded offset of 21 feet was on a road near the visitor center. In most places, the roads, buildings, and fences that were offset have been repaired so that evidence of the offset is obscure. However, on the Earthquake Trail you will see where the 1906 fault offset a fence by 17 feet, then cut along a hillside and sliced the corner off the Skinner Barn. The fence has been reconstructed to show the offset. Posts show where the fault cut along the hillside toward the Skinner Barn.

The posts mark the trace of the fault line that was formed during the 1906 San Francisco Earthquake. This fault cut through the corner of the old Skinner barn in the center of the photo, but the barn has been rebuilt.

Rift Zone Trail: If you have time to make this 4.4-mile hike, you will be walking along the San Andreas fault zone for the entire distance. If you can arrange it, get dropped off at the Five Brooks trailhead and walk north to the visitor center. While on this trip you will see some of the topography characteristic of the San Andreas fault zone, especially the linear ridges and meadows formed from sag ponds that have been filled in. During the wet season, the trail is often wet and muddy due to the poor and interrupted drainage along the fault zone. Three miles north of the trailhead the trail passes "The Oaks", an old Victorian house that was built in 1869 and survived the 1906 earthquake without serious damage.

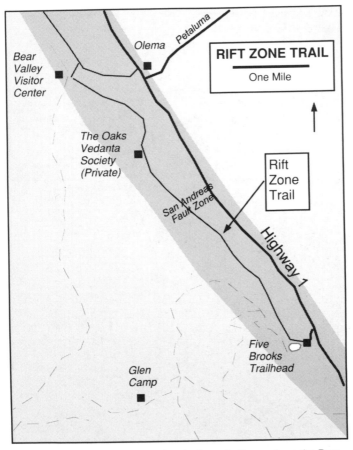

The Rift Zone Trail follows the San Andreas fault zone from the Bear Valley visitor center to the Five Brooks trailhead.

Point Reyes Headlands

The Point Reyes Headlands jut out southward into the Pacific from the Point Reyes Peninsula and intercept the full fury of the large Pacific waves. The headlands have survived this onslaught because they are made up of very hard granite and conglomerate. The granite forms the backbone of the headlands and the conglomerate caps the east and west tips of the headlands. You will see the granite at the Sea Lion Overlook and the conglomerate at the Point Reyes Lighthouse. To reach the Point Reyes Headlands from the Bear Valley visitor center, go north on Bear Valley Road. At 1.8 miles it changes to Sir Francis Drake Highway. Continue north on Sir Francis Drake Highway 18.7 miles to the parking area for the Point Reyes Lighthouse.

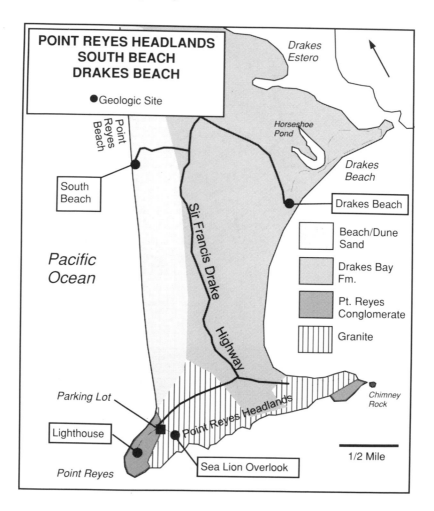

● *Sea Lion Overlook*

To get to the Sea Lion Overlook, go to the south end of the parking lot for the Point Reyes Lighthouse and take the path about 100 yards to the overlook. The rock that is exposed along the path and at the overlook is granite. The granite is light-colored and is composed of coarse grains that have sharp edges. If you examine a fresh piece of this granite with a magnifying glass, you will see that most of the grains are about the size of a small pea and that there are several types of grains. Most of the grains are feldspar. The feldspar grains are white or milky and have flat surfaces that reflect light. Feldspar is a very common mineral found in many different types of igneous rocks. The next most common mineral is quartz, which appears as light gray translucent grains with curved fractures. The quartz fills the irregular spaces between the other grains, since the quartz was still liquid after the other minerals had crystallized. Hornblende appears as black elongated rods with striations, and makes up about 10% of the rock. Mica appears as small shiny plates, some black and some light colored.

This granite is similar to the granite at Montara Mountain, and is part of the large Salinian block that was transported northward from the southern Sierras by the San Andreas fault. The Salinian block, which includes most of the granitic basement rocks west of the San Andreas fault and north of Santa Cruz, was discussed in more detail at the Devils Slide locality during the trip to the Bay Area faults.

Most of the granite in the Salinian block was formed in Cretaceous time while the Franciscan subduction zone was active. The granite was formed during the subduction process. Rocks carried into the subduction zone were heated to form a silica-rich magma and this magma was then intruded into the overlying rocks. The magma did not reach the surface of the ground, but cooled slowly under a blanket of rocks several miles thick. Because the granite cooled slowly, the large crystals that are characteristic of granite had time to form.

Although the entire Point Reyes Peninsula is underlain by granite, it is covered by younger sedimentary rocks in most places. It is exposed only in the Point Reyes Headlands, along the Inverness Ridge, and at Tomales Point. Most of the granite along the Inverness Ridge is weathered to a depth of about 30 feet and looks like coarse sand where exposed in road cuts.

●*Lighthouse*

The conglomerate that caps the east and west tips of the Point Reyes Headlands is of Paleocene age, and is referred to as the *Point Reyes Conglomerate*. This conglomerate is well exposed along the path from the parking area to the Point Reyes Lighthouse and visitor center. The visitor center is an easy 0.5-mile walk from the parking area. From the visitor center you can go down the 308 steps to the lighthouse. The cliffs below the lighthouse are the home to thousands of common murres. You may also see sea lions on the offshore rocks, and gray whales during their migration from January to April. The lighthouse and visitor center are open Thursday through Monday, weather permitting. Expect wind, and dress warmly. For information phone 415-669-1534.

In exposures of the conglomerate near the visitor center you will see that the conglomerate occurs in beds that are from one- to ten-feet thick that are interlayered with beds of sandstone that are several feet thick. The conglomerate is composed of pebbles and boulders of granite, volcanic rocks and chert in a matrix of coarse sand. Some of the boulders are several feet in diameter. The largest boulders are usually granite. The granite boulders were derived from the same granitic rocks that form the basement of the Point Reyes Peninsula. The conglomerate is extremely hard and has resisted weathering and erosion. Indeed, if it were not for the armor plating provided by this conglomerate there would probably be no Point Reyes Headlands.

The Point Reyes Conglomerate is found nowhere else on the Point Reyes Peninsula. However, conglomerate of the same age and with the same types of boulders occurs near the Monterey Peninsula, 100 miles to the south. It is likely that the Point Reyes Conglomerate and the conglomerate near the Monterey Peninsula are the same conglomerate, and that the Point Reyes Conglomerate was carried northward from the Monterey area by the San Gregorio fault, one of the many faults of the San Andreas fault system.

The granite and the Paleocene conglomerate in the Monterey area are on the west side of the San Andreas fault, so the rocks in both of these areas have been moved north a considerable distance by the San Andreas fault. However, the rocks on the west side of the San Gregorio fault got an extra 100-mile shove by the San Gregorio fault, like one slow tramp steamer passing another going in the same direction.

The Point Reyes Lighthouse is built on the Point Reyes Conglomerate. This conglomerate is extremely hard and has resisted erosion so that it now forms the east and west tips of the Point Reyes Headlands.

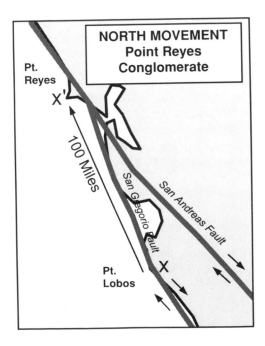

NORTH MOVEMENT
Point Reyes
Conglomerate

Pt. Reyes

X'

100 Miles

San Gregorio Fault

San Andreas Fault

Pt. Lobos

X

Conglomerate that is similar to the Point Reyes Conglomerate is found at Point Lobos near Monterey. It is likely that the Point Reyes Conglomerate was deposited in the Monterey area and then moved 100 miles north by the San Gregorio fault, from **X** to **X'**. The San Gregorio fault is part of the San Andreas fault system and was probably active earlier than the San Andreas fault.

South Beach

South Beach, which lies at the south end of Point Reyes Beach, faces directly into the prevailing northwest winds. This results in some of the largest waves along the entire California coast. To reach South Beach from Point Reyes Headlands, follow Sir Francis Drake Highway 4.8 miles to the turn-off to South Beach, then follow the road 0.8 miles to the parking area. The pounding surf and rip currents are very dangerous, so stay away from the water. Also check the tide table before walking on the beach so that you will not get trapped by the high tide.

●South Beach

South Beach has been carved into the soft rocks of the Drakes Bay Formation. It would seem that the gigantic waves at South Beach should rapidly erode the soft rocks of the Drakes Bay Formation. However, this erosion has been slowed down by the large amount of sand on the beach. Much of the wave energy is spent in moving this beach sand from one place to another and back again. In winter, gigantic storm waves remove sand from the beach and place it offshore in bars that run parallel to the beach. The winter waves then break on these bars and the beach is protected from the full onslaught of the waves. In summer, the smaller waves remove the sand from the offshore bars and place it back on the beach, building the beach back up. This sand movement is typical of many beaches. Much of this sand would probably like to escape this constant thrashing, but it finds it difficult to get around Tomales Point and Point Reyes. It is thus held firmly on Point Reyes Beach to stoically endure its fate of eternal beatings. The beach sand does, however, have one method of escape: it can become airborne in the strong prevailing winds and escape from the beach to become part of a sand dune. The major fields of sand dunes on the Point Reyes Peninsula are directly inland from Point Reyes Beach and are made up of sand that has escaped from the beach in this manner. Most of the sand dunes along the California coastline occur at the south end of sandy beaches where the sand has been driven by the prevailing northwesterly winds.

If you look at the sand from South Beach with a magnifying glass, you will see that it is composed of many different types of grains. Some are clear and others are yellow, red, black, brown, or green. The sand grains are made up of opal, quartzite, chert, granite and conglomerate. Most of the grains are highly polished and well rounded due to the constant reworking by the waves. It is unusual for sand to be composed of this many different types of grains. Obviously the sand was derived from a great variety of igneous, sedimentary and metamorphic rocks.

South Beach faces directly into the prevailing northwesterly winds and has some of the largest waves on the California coast. The sand on this beach is composed of many different types of grains, suggesting a variety of source areas for the sand.

The sea cliffs at Drakes Beach consist of siltstone and very fine-grained sandstone of the Drakes Bay Formation. Drakes Beach is on the protected leeward side of the peninsula so that the waves are smaller and the beach sand is very fine grained.

Drakes Beach

The white cliffs that form the backdrop for Drakes Beach consist of siltstones and mudstones of the Drakes Bay Formation. These cliffs reminded Sir Francis Drake of the white cliffs of southeast England when he stopped here in 1579 to make repairs of the *Golden Hind* before continuing across the Pacific on his circumnavigation of the globe. You can get a good look at these sea cliffs at Drakes Beach.

The turnoff to Drakes Beach is on Sir Francis Drake Highway 5.3 miles north of the parking lot for the Point Reyes Lighthouse. Follow the access road 1.7 miles to the Kenneth C. Patrick visitor center. The visitor center has exhibits on the plant and animal life of Drakes Bay and on 16th Century exploration during the period of Sir Francis Drake's visit. It is open weekends and holidays. For information, phone 415-669-1250.

●Drakes Beach

The Drakes Bay Formation is well exposed in the sea cliffs adjacent to the visitor center. The sedimentary rocks in the sea cliffs consist mainly of claystone, siltstone and fine-grained sandstone, and these rocks occur in near-horizontal beds from several inches to several feet thick. The claystone is like hard mud. The siltstone is composed of very small grains that feel gritty, but are to small to see. The fine-grained sandstone is composed of very small sand grains, but you can see the individual grains without a magnifying glass. All of these rocks are very soft and can be easily broken by hand. Note that the beach sand here is very fine grained, since it was derived from these fine-grained sedimentary rocks.

The sedimentary rocks of the Drakes Bay Formation were deposited in an ocean basin during Pliocene time from two to five million years ago. This ocean basin once covered most of the Point Reyes Peninsula. However, the rocks along most of the edges of that basin have been eroded, so we do not know the exact extent of the basin. Fish and marine vertebrates lived in that ocean and left some of their remains as fossils. These fossils mainly occur in the claystone at the base of the formation. A total thickness of about 1500 feet of sediments accumulated in the basin.

The rocks of the Drakes Bay Formation are similar to the Purisma Formation in the Santa Cruz Mountains, and it is likely that the Drakes Bay Formation was deposited when the peninsula was in the area of the Santa Cruz Mountains.

Bolinas

Bolinas is a small town that lies at the mouth of the Bolinas Lagoon on the west side of the San Andreas fault. There are two geologic sites near the town, the Bolinas bluff where you will see the siltstones and sandstones of the Merced Formation and Agate Beach where you will see the Monterey Shale. The people of Bolinas have a reputation of being somewhat private, to the extent that there are few road signs advising you of the existence of the town. However, once you find your way there, the town is very scenic and worth a trip on its own.

●*Bolinas Bluff*

To get to the Bolinas bluff, follow Highway 1 to the Olema-Bolinas Road, 9.5 miles south of Olema, then go south on the Olema-Bolinas Road. At 2.0 miles from the turnoff you will reach the town of Bolinas. Continue through the town 0.5 miles to the parking area for the beach near the mouth of Bolinas Lagoon. Walk west along the beach a couple of hundred feet to where the rocks that form the bluff are well-exposed.

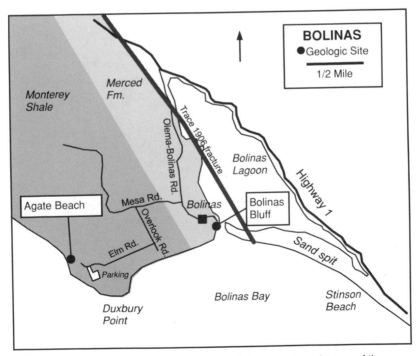

The bluff near the town of Bolinas consists of siltstones and sandstones of the Merced Formation. The bluff at Agate Beach is formed from the Monterey Shale.

The bluff at Bolinas consists of soft sand and silt of the Merced Formation. The siltstone contains some layers of shale with concretions that contain fossils. These sediments were deposited in a nearly closed-in bay along the west side of the San Francisco peninsula in late Pliocene and early Pleistocene time. This bay had the misfortune of lying across the San Andreas fault. After the rocks were deposited, the sediments that had been deposited on the east side of the fault remained in the San Francisco area near Fort Funston and the sediments that had been deposited on the west side of the fault were carried north by the fault to their present location at Bolinas.

The San Andreas fault goes directly through the Bolinas Lagoon, and is responsible for the lagoon. The Stinson Beach spit lies across the mouth of the lagoon and can easily be seen from the bluff at Bolinas. During the Great San Francisco Earthquake of 1906, the western tip of the spit was offset several feet to the north by the active trace of the fault.

●Agate Beach

The Monterey Shale was deposited in Miocene time and is one of the most widespread and distinctive sedimentary units in the Coast Ranges of central California. These rocks cover much of the south part of the Point Reyes Peninsula and are well-exposed in the sea cliffs from Drakes Bay south to Duxbury Point. Agate Beach is one of the best places on the peninsula to get a look at the Monterey Shale.

To get to Agate Beach from Bolinas, go north on the Olema-Bolinas Road 0.5 miles to Mesa Road and follow Mesa Road 0.6 miles to the west, turn left on Overbrook Road, go 0.5 miles, then turn right on Elm Road and go 0.9 miles to the parking area for Agate Beach County Park. Follow the path to the beach. The Monterey Shale is exposed in the cliffs along the beach.

When you look at these rocks in detail, you will see that they consist almost entirely of very thin-bedded shale. The shale readily breaks into small sharp fragments and is easily eroded by the waves. From Agate Beach south to Duxbury Point, wave action has cut a broad platform near sea level, as if the rocks had been cut off horizontally by a chain saw. There are a number of small, thin ridges on the surface of this wave-cut platform. The ridges represent the edges of the steeply dipping beds of shale. From Agate Beach you can see these thin ridges of shale extending southward to form Duxbury Point and Duxbury Reef.

This photo, which looks south from Agate Beach toward Duxbury Reef, shows thin beds of Monterey Shale tilted steeply to the right.

Further north toward Drakes Bay much of the Monterey Shale is very rich in silica. The shale picked up this extra silica from widespread volcanic activity that occurred while the sediments were being deposited. Fine silica-rich volcanic ash thrown into the atmosphere from erupting Miocene volcanoes fell into the ocean waters and then settled on the sea floor where it formed beds of chert and silica-rich shale. The volcanic ash also saturated the seawater with silica so that small silica-rich aquatic plants, called diatoms, became abundant. These diatoms settled onto the sea floor to form beds of punky shale. The punky shales are white and very light weight. They look somewhat like chalk; however, chalk is formed from skeletons of soft calcium carbonate rather than the hard silica.

These rocks are very distinctive because of the silica-rich shale and punky shale. You can see good exposures of the Monterey Shale at the Point Arena Lighthouse 90 miles to the north, at Natural Bridges State Park near Santa Cruz, and at Shell Beach in San Luis Obispo County.

ACKNOWLEDGMENTS

Thanks to all of the people that were involved in the preparation and completion of this book. This includes the many nongeologist that have asked good penetrating questions during local geologic hikes as well as the park personnel and staff at the many localities visited during the geologic trips.

Special thanks to Bob Lorentzen of Bored Feet Publications and Liz Petersen of Petersen Graphics for help in the design, editing, publication and printing of the book, and to Lucie Marshall for editing of the manuscript.

Eyewitness Account, 1868 Hayward Earthquake
"The crack past out diagonally up the Haywards Hill and crost 3 feet from the south corner of the old hotel, past just east of the Odd Fellows' Building, through the Castro lot, tearing off a corner of the adobe house which stood where the jail now is, on through Walpert's Hill toward Decoto. By the hotel the crack first opened 18 to 20 inches, but soon closed to 5 or 6. It was of unknown depth: several balls of twine, tied together, with an iron sinker, failed to find bottom. There was no water in the fissure, for the iron came up dry. From the corner of B and First Streets another crack past nearly eastward toward the hills, and faded out by the sulfur spring about 1.5 miles distant. In a general way, the crack from Hawards to beyond Decoto past from 100 to 300 feet above the base of the hills. Practically not a house was left on its foundations in Haywards. ..."

AFTERWORD

As I mentioned in the Preface, I have drawn on the work of many geologists in preparing this book. I would like to acknowledge several of the sources that I leaned on particularly heavily. Clyde Wahrhaftig's *A Streetcar to Subduction and other Plate Tectonic Trips by Public Transport in San Francisco* provides detailed geologic descriptions not only of many parts of San Francisco, but also of the Marin Headlands, Angel Island, and the Hayward fault. The mysteries of the Franciscan rocks of California are covered in detail in California Division of Mines and Geology Bulletin 183, edited by Edgar Bailey, William Irwin, and David Jones, and in Special Publication 114, edited by Peter Schiffman and David Wagner. U.S.G.S. Professional Paper 1515, edited by Robert Wallace, is a must for anyone wanting more detail on the San Andreas fault. The report by Andy Lawson on *The California Earthquake of April 18, 1906*, now known as the Great San Francisco Earthquake, is a classic, and is available in reprint. This report is packed with detailed information on the San Francisco earthquake. California Division of Mines and Geology Special Publication 104, edited by Stephen McNutt and Robert Snydor, has a number of articles that cover many different aspects of the Loma Prieta Earthquake. There were a number of helpful field trip guides in several publications of the California Division of Mines and Geology, especially Special Publication 109, edited by Doris Sloan and David Wagner, and Bulletin 190, edited by Edgar Bailey. John McPhee's book, *Assembling California*, gives a very readable and enjoyable discussion of plate tectonics. If you want to know more about earthquakes, read Bruce Bolt's book, *Earthquakes*, and if you want to know what's going to happen to your house in an earthquake, read Peter Yanev's book, *Peace of Mind in Earthquake Country*.

Whether you are a nongeologist, a beginning geologist, or an experienced geologist, I must warn you that the geology of the San Francisco area is complex and not all geologists will agree with all of the geologic explanations in this book. So be it. I have presented what seems to me, at this time, the most reasonable explanation, and have not burdened the reader with all of the various alternatives. If you see something that is incorrect or misleading, please let me know. I'm not easily offended and would be pleased to get your thoughts.

FURTHER READING

There are many excellent articles and books about the geology, faults and earthquakes of northern California and the San Francisco area. Following are a few that are of special interest. Most of these are easily available at bookstores and libraries. Many of these contain more detailed references for the geologist wishing more information.

Alt, D.D. and Hyndman D.W., 1975, *Roadside Geology of Northern California*, Mountain Press Publishing Co., Missoula, Montana, 244 p.

Bailey, E.H., Irwin, W., and Jones, D., eds., 1964, *Franciscan and Related Rocks and their Significance in the Geology of Western California*, California Division of Mines and Geology Bulletin 183, 177 p.

Bailey, E.H., ed., 1966, *Geology of Northern California*, California Division of Mines and Geology Bulletin 190, 508 p.

Bolt, B.A., 1993, *Earthquakes*, W.H. Freeman and Company, N.Y., 331 p.

Galloway, A.J., 1977, *Geology of the Point Reyes Peninsula, Marin County, California*, California Division of Mines and Geology, Bulletin 202, 72 p.

Howard, A.D., 1979, *Geologic History of Middle California*, University of California Press, Berkeley, 113 p.

Lawson, A. C., chairman, 1908, *The California Earthquake of April 18, 1906, Report of the State Earthquake Investigation Commission*, Carnegie Institution of Washington Publication 87, 2 v.

McNutt, S. and Sydnor, R.H., 1990, *The Loma Prieta (Santa Cruz Mountains), California Earthquake of October 17, 1989*, California Division of Mines and Geology, Special Publication 104, 142 p.

McPhee, J., 1993, *Assembling California*, Farrar, Straus and Giroux, N.Y., 304 p.

Norris, R.M. and Webb, R.W., 1990, *Geology of California*, John Wiley & Sons, Inc., N.Y., 541 p.

Schiffman, P. and Wagner, D.L., eds., 1992, *Field Guide to the Geology and Metamorphism of the Franciscan Complex and Western Metamorphic Belt of Northern California,* California Division of Mines and Geology Special Publication 114, 78 p.

Sloan, D. and Wagner, D.L., eds., 1991, *Geologic Excursions in Northern California: San Francisco to the Sierra Nevada,* California Division of Mines and Geology Special Publication 109, 130 p.

Smelser, M.G., 1987, *Geology of the Mussel Rock Landslike, San Mateo County,* California Geology, v. 41, p. 59-66.

Vedder, J. G. and Wallace, R. E., 1970, *Map Showing Recently Active Breaks along the San Andreas and Related Faults between Cholame Valley and Tejon Pass, California,* U. S. Geological Survey Miscellaneous Geologic Investigations Map I-574, scale 1:24,000.

Wahrhaftig, C., 1984, *A Streetcar to Subduction and other Plate Tectonic Trips by Public Transport in San Francisco,* American Geophysical Union, Washington, D.C., 76 p.

Wallace, R.E., ed., 1990, *The San Andreas Fault System, California,* U.S. Geological Survey Professional Paper 1515, 283 p.

Yanev, P.I., 1991, *Peace of Mind in Earthquake Country,* Chronicle Books, San Francisco, California, 218 p.

GLOSSARY

agglomerate: a volcanic rock consisting mainly of rounded volcanic fragments.

alluvium: sediment deposited by streams, mainly sand, silt, gravel and clay.

amphiboles: a group of common rock forming silicate minerals rich in iron and magnesium; typically form dark elongated crystals.

anticline: an arched-up fold of rock. In most anticlines the oldest rocks are in the center and the beds dip away from the crest.

aragonite: a mineral formed of calcium carbonate, similar to calcite, but usually with good prismatic cleavage.

basalt: a dark gray or greenish gray fine-grained volcanic rock. Basalt forms the earth's crust under most of the world's oceans.

batholith: a large mass of granitic rocks, with an outcrop area greater than 40 miles.

bed: smallest layer of sedimentary rock, usually formed during one depositional event.

biotite: black mica.

blueschist: a schist, often blue colored, containing blue amphiboles such as lawsonite, glaucophane or crossite; these schists form only in subduction zones under conditions of very high pressure and abnormally low temperature.

blueschist facies: refers to a group of rocks that have been subjected to the degree of metamorphism that form blueschists.

carnelian: a translucent red or orange variety of chalcedony, a cryptocrystalline type of quartz.

chert: a fine-grained, hard, silica-rich rock that usually occurs as thin layers or concretions. Chert may be colored white, black, gray, red, green, brown or yellow.

chlorite: a soft, green, platy silicate mineral containing iron, magnesium and aluminum; typically forms at low temperature and low pressure, often as an alteration product of iron-magnesium minerals.

claystone: a sedimentary rock consisting of clay minerals, but without the partings of shale.

concretion: a hard ball-shaped mass formed in a sedimentary bed by localized precipitation resulting from a tendency of minerals of like composition to precipitate around a common center.

conglomerate: a sedimentary rock consisting of boulders, cobbles and pebbles in a sand matrix.

convection currents: currents within the heavy viscous rocks of the earth's mantle that move the continental and oceanic plates that cover the surface of the earth.

cross bedding: inclined layers within a sedimentary bed.

crossite: a dark-blue, sodium-rich mineral close in composition to glaucophane; characteristic of the blueschist facies of metamorphism.

crust: the outer layer of the earth. Oceanic crust is mainly basalt and about five-miles thick. Continental crust is typically granitic, and about 25-miles thick.

deposition: the process of laying down sedimentary rocks.

diabase: a fine-grained igneous rock that has the same chemical composition as gabbro and basalt; it differs from basalt in that it was not extruded onto the earth's surface.

diatoms: one-celled aquatic plants that have a shell of silica.

earthquake: shaking of the earth due to movement along a fault.

eclogite: an unusual, heavy, dark-green metamorphic rock that contains garnet and sodium-rich pyroxene. Eclogites are formed only at abnormally low temperatures and high pressures and are considered as indicators of subduction zones.

erosion: the wearing away of the earth's landscape by natural forces of water, waves, ice, or wind.

estuary: the tidal mouth of a river valley, usually has a mixture of fresh water and salt water.

exotic block: a block of rock in a melange that is strikingly different from the matrix of the melange and other common rocks in the melange.

fan: a fan-shaped mass of sedimentary rock.

fault: a fracture in the earth's crust along which the opposite sides have been offset.

feldspar: a common group of rock-forming minerals found in many igneous and metamorphic rocks. Feldspars are colorless, white or pink, and consist of aluminum silicates with various quantities of potassium, sodium or calcium. Feldspars rich in potassium are commonly referred to as orthoclase or K-feldspar and those rich in sodium and/or calcium as plagioclase feldspar.

formation: a distinct mappable body of rock, usually named for the geographic locality where it was described. Formations can be subdivided into members.

fossil: organic remains, shells, skeletons, prints, buried by natural processes and preserved in the rocks.

gabbro: a coarse-grained igneous rock of the same chemical composition as basalt. Gabbro cooled slowly at depth rather than rapidly on the surface like basalt.

garnet: a group of metamorphic minerals, usually red and commonly forming twelve-sided crystals.

glacial, interglacial: a glacial period is a climatic episode in which very large glaciers develop. The glaciers recede during interglacial periods. There have been at least four major glacial periods during the last three million years.

glaucophane: a blue mineral that occurs as silky blue fibers or dark blue needles in metamorphic rocks formed at high pressure and abnormally low temperature; typically results from metamorphism of sodium-rich igneous rocks.

granite: a coarse-grained light colored igneous rock rich in quartz and feldspar, usually contains minor amounts of biotite and hornblende.

graywacke: a sandstone with a high proportion of feldspar, rock fragments, and matrix.

greenstone: a dark green volcanic rock. The green color is due mainly to chlorite and other minerals that were formed by low-grade metamorphism of the volcanic rock.

hornblende: a shiny black mineral common to many igneous and metamorphic rocks; commonly occurs in the rock as columns or elongated blades with striations.

igneous rocks: rocks that have solidified from molten rock. Includes both volcanic and plutonic rocks. Volcanic rocks solidified on or near the earth's surface. Plutonic rocks solidified deep in the earth.

interbedded: alternating beds.

isostatic: a condition of equilibrium, similar to floating, of the lithosphere above the mantle.

jadeite: a very dense sodium-bearing pyroxene formed by alteration of sodium-rich plagioclase at high pressure.

K-feldspar: see feldspar.

lawsonite: a pale blue hydrated calcium-aluminum silicate with the composition of calcium plagioclase plus water. Lawsonite has a high density and is formed only at high pressure and abnormally low temperature.

liquefaction: the process by which unconsolidated sediments change into a fluid state.

lithosphere: the outer rigid part of the earth; usually about 60 miles thick. Continental and oceanic crust represent the upper part of the lithosphere.

magma: molten rock, formed by heating of rocks below the earth's surface.

mantle: the part of the earth between the base of the lithosphere and the earth's core at a depth of 1800 miles. The mantle is composed of ultramafic rocks, mainly pyroxene and olivine.

marine sediment: a sedimentary rock deposited in the sea.

melange: a mixture of angular blocks in a clay matrix formed by intense shearing action in a subduction zone.

member: a subdivision of a formation.

metamorphic rock: a rock that has been formed from an earlier igneous or sedimentary rock by the action of heat, pressure or hot water solutions, usually deep within the earth's crust.

mica: a common potassium-containing mineral found as small shiny flakes in many granitic and metamorphic rocks. Muscovite is white mica and biotite is black mica.

mineral: a naturally occurring inorganic substance composed of crystalline chemical elements or compounds. Common minerals include quartz, feldspar, hornblende, and pyroxene.

mudstone: indurated mud; lacks the fissility of shale.

nonmarine: sedimentary rocks not deposited in marine waters. Includes lake beds, river deposits, and sand dunes.

olivine: a green iron-magnesium silicate commonly found in ultramafic rocks and as scattered crystals in some basalt and gabbro.

ophiolite: igneous rocks of the earth's oceanic crust. A typical ophiolite sequence includes, from top to base, pillow basalts, diabase dikes, gabbro, serpentine and ultramafic rocks.

orthoclase: see feldspar.

P wave: the primary or fastest earthquake wave; travels through the rocks by a series of compressions and dilations of the rock.

pillow basalt: a basalt that has formed under water; characterized by the formation of pillows.

plagioclase: see feldspar.

plate: a discrete segment of the earth's lithosphere that moves as a unit as if it were rigid.

plate tectonics: the concept that the outer part of the earth is composed of a number of plates that move horizontally over geologic time. The plates are moved by convection currents in the earth's mantle. Major geologic features of the earth's crust are formed along plate margins.

pyroxene: a group of silicate minerals found in many igneous and metamorphic rocks. Pyroxenes typically contain calcium, sodium, iron and magnesium. Pyroxene crystals are usually short and stout.

pyroxenite: a dark, heavy rock composed mainly of pyroxenes.

quartz: a very common mineral composed of silicon dioxide. Quartz occurs in igneous, sedimentary and metamorphic rocks, and also as veins in all of these rocks. Quartz is typically translucent or glassy. It is extremely hard and resistant to weathering, and is a major component of most sandstone.

radiolaria: microscopic one-celled floating marine animals with shells of silica.

regression: seaward movement of the shoreline.

rock: a hard naturally occurring material composed of one or more minerals. The major rock categories are igneous, sedimentary and metamorphic.

S wave: the secondary or slowest earthquake wave; travels through the rock as a series of vibrations transverse to the direction of travel.

sag pond: a body of water occupying a depression created by movement of the earth's surface along a fault zone.

sandstone: a sedimentary rock composed of sand-sized particles.

schist: a foliated coarse-grained metamorphic rock that tends to break into platy fragments.

schistose sandstone: a sandstone that has been metamorphosed to the degree that it has some of the characteristics of schist, but the original sandstone character is still apparent.

sediments: rock fragments transported and deposited mainly by wind or water, to form layers of loose rock, such as mud, silt and sand.

sedimentary basin: a low area in the earth's crust where sediments accumulate.

sedimentary rock: a layered rock composed of consolidated sediments. Common sedimentary rocks include conglomerate, sandstone, siltstone and shale. May also include rocks precipitated from solutions, like salt, and rocks composed of organic remains, like limestone.

seismograph: an instrument that detects and records earthquakes.

serpentine: a dense, dark green rock formed by the alteration of ultramafic rocks in the earth's mantle by hot water solutions.

shale: a sedimentary rock consisting largely of clay minerals. It has a finely laminated structure which gives it a fissility along which the rock tends to split readily.

silicate: a mineral containing silica and oxygen along with other elements. Most of the earth's crust consists of minerals that are silicates.

siliceous: consisting largely of silica (silicon dioxide), especially noncrystalline silica, such as opal.

silt, siltstone: sediment or sedimentary rock composed of grains smaller than sand and bigger than clay.

slickentite: serpentine that is highly foliated and splits along the foliation surfaces.

spreading center: the zone along which plates are pulled apart by upwelling convection currents in the earth's mantle.

subduction zone: the zone along which an oceanic plate descends into the earth's mantle.

subsidence: lowering of the earth's crust by tectonic forces within the earth. Sedimentary basins tend to form in these areas.

syncline: a downward fold of rocks. Typically the youngest rocks are in the center and the rocks on the flanks dip toward the center.

terrace: a flat or gently sloping bench that is the remnant of an old coastline.

terrace deposits: sedimentary rocks deposited on a terrace.

terrane: a large rock unit brought to its present location by plate movement. The terrane may have traveled thousands of miles to get to its present location, may differ considerably from adjacent terranes, and its place of origin may be unknown.

thrust: a nearly horizontal fault in which the upper plate has been placed over the lower plate.

transform fault: a fault that offsets spreading centers.

transgression: landward movement of the shoreline.

tuff: a rock composed of compacted volcanic ash.

turbidite: sediments that were deposited by a turbidity current.

turbidity current: a current of dense water and sediment that flows rapidly down the slope of the sea floor, like an underwater avalanche.

ultramafic: a rock that contains a superabundance of heavy, dark minerals rich in magnesium and iron silicates, mainly olivine and pyroxene, and little or no feldspar.

uplift: upward movement of the earth's crust. If the uplifted area is above sea level, the uplifted area will be subjected to erosion and will supply sediments to sedimentary basins.

vesicle: a small cavity formed in a volcanic rock by expanding gas as the rock solidifies.

volcanic: igneous rocks that solidified near the earth's surface, usually fine-grained.

weathering: the alteration of a rock as a result of conditions at the earth's surface, usually involving reaction with water, atmospheric gasses, and organic products. In humid areas weathering normally results in the formation of soil.

INDEX

Order Form

Geologic Trips, San Francisco and the Bay Area

To order additional copies of this book, send order to:

GeoPress
P.O. Box 964
Gualala, CA 95445-0964

Book: $13.95
Shipping and handling: $3.00 per order.
Include sales tax for books shipped to California addresses.

No. of books: _____
Remittance: $_____

Payment should be by check made out to GeoPress and enclosed with your order.

Send book to:
Name:_____
Address:_____
City:_____ State:_____ Zip:_____